# SCOTTISH GENEALOGY:

## The Basics and Beyond

D1603769

# SCOTTISH GENEALOGY:

## The Basics and Beyond

## David Dobson

Genealogical Publishing Co., Inc.

ISBN 9780806321134


Text Layout and Cover Design by Kate Boyer, Heron and Earth Design
Main text set in Adobe Garamond Pro, headings in Bodoni 72

Cover Landscape photo courtesy of Marian & Brent Hoffman
Gravestone Image, Abraham gravestone – Lundie Graveyard, Angus

# CONTENTS

# ILLUSTRATIONS

# ABBREVIATIONS USED
in source citations in this book

| | |
|---|---|
| AA | Angus Archives |
| ACA | Aberdeen City Archives |
| AUL | Aberdeen University Library/Archives |
| AYA | Ayrshire Archives |
| BA | Borders Archives |
| DCA | Dundee City Archives |
| DUA | Dundee University Archives |
| ECA | Edinburgh City Archives |
| FA | Fife Archives |
| FDCA | Friends of the Dundee City Archives |
| GCA | Glasgow City Archives |
| HA | Highland Archives |
| NLS | National Library of Scotland |
| NRAS | National Register of Archives |
| NRS | National Records of Scotland |
| PKA | Perth and Kinross Archive |
| SA | Stirling Council Archives |
| SAUL | St Andrews University Library/Archives |
| SGS | Scottish Genealogy Society |
| SHS | Scottish History Society |
| TNA | The National Archives (UK) |
| TVFHS | Tay Valley Family History Society |
| ZA | Shetland Archives |

# INTRODUCTION

Beyond the basic record genealogy sources in Scotland—civil records, church records, and censuses—there is a wide and rich range of family history material available in both publications and manuscripts, which can be used to add more detail to the facts your research in basic sources produces. This book identifies the major sources and repositories for those just starting their Scottish genealogy research, but what makes this publication stand out from other Scottish genealogy guidebooks is its goal to highlight for more advanced researchers the other, less commonly used, sources that exist. Once family history researchers have established the basic information on their ancestor's birth or baptism, marriage, and death, the task will be "to put flesh on the skeleton" of known facts.

With an emphasis on publications, manuscript sources, and archival records, this book presents ways to trace ancestors using alternative sources, concentrating on sources predominantly between 1550 and 1850. Religious denominations in Scotland, occupational lists, military and maritime sources, emigration records, burgh records, and rural records, such as those of baronies, are all covered. The many published sources listed will enable researchers to put the basic facts they have gathered into context.

If your ancestor had a skilled trade or craft, it is likely there are records of apprenticeships that should be followed up. Certain professions would have required university training. All the ministers of the church, for example, were expected to have graduated from one of the old Scottish universities, which kept excellent records (many of which have been published); medical practitioners were either apprenticed or were university educated, as were lawyers (alias writers). It should be noted that some Scots went to continental universities, especially Leiden in the Netherlands, for classes in law or medicine. Ideally researchers should work from original documents and note the source as a reference to the data; for example, National Records of Scotland documents should be preceded by NRS; National Library of Scotland manuscript references should be preceded by NLS; and the U.S. National Archives and Records Administration references should be preceded by NARA.

Beware of unreferenced material, particularly on the internet, as some of it is wishful thinking or based on hearsay. Even normally reliable sources can be wrong. For many years sources like the *Dictionary of National Biography* stated that "William Kidd (the pirate or privateer) was born in Greenock, Scotland, son of a minister." Years ago, I came across a transcript of a trial in London before the High Court of the Admiralty of England, where Kidd was a witness in 1695. He stated that he was born in Dundee, aged 41, a mariner based in New York. This clearly was at odds with the traditional story, so I decided to check it out. Back in Dundee I checked the baptismal register of the Dundee parish church and found that he had been baptized there in 1654, the son of John Kidd, a seaman, and his wife, Bessie Butchart. I then went to the city archives, and in the local seabox I found a reference to John and a few years later to his wife, who was in receipt of a pension, which implied that John had perished at sea. The traditional story was that William's father was a minister of the Church of Scotland (the only church at the time), so I turned to the *Fastii Scoticannae*, which provides biographical data on every minister of the Church of Scotland since the Reformation of 1560, but no Kidd was mentioned in Greenock or anywhere in Scotland. So, the traditional story that Kidd was born in Greenock, the son of a minister of the church, was wrong; he, in fact, came from more humble origins in Dundee. So do not rely on unreferenced sources!

This book is the culmination of over fifty years of historical and genealogical research in archives and libraries throughout Scotland. My commitment to Scottish family history resulted in my returning to academia, this time to study Scottish History and the Scottish Diaspora. Initially I enrolled at the University of St. Andrews, where I studied for a Master of Philosophy degree entitled "Scottish Emigration to Colonial America, 1607–1785," a thesis that was published by the University of Georgia Press. Later I enrolled at the University of Aberdeen to study for a Ph.D. My thesis was on "Scottish Trade with Colonial Charleston, 1683-1783," which was published in Glasgow and subsequently in Baltimore by the Clearfield Company. I should like to take this opportunity to thank the Genealogical Publishing Company and its subsidiary, the Clearfield Company, for publishing most of my genealogical source books over many years, and especially Michael Tepper and Joseph Garonzik for their encouragement and practical advice over many years.

*David Dobson, Dundee, Scotland, 2020*

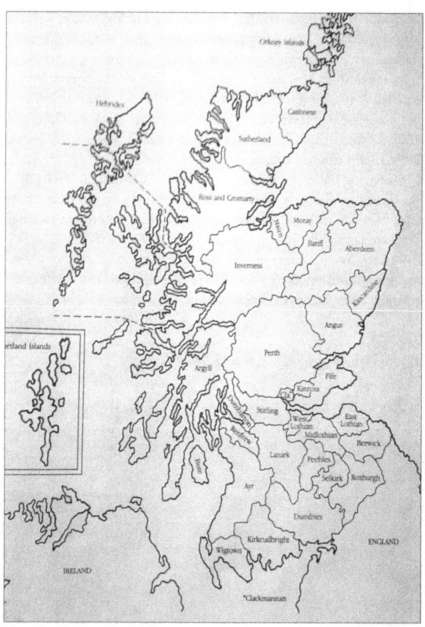

Map of historical counties

Chapter 1
# GETTING STARTED

The basic sources for Scottish Genealogical Research are the Old Parish Registers of the Church of Scotland, now supplemented by the records of the Roman Catholic Church in Scotland; the Decennial Censuses of Scotland between 1841 and 1911; and the Statutory Registers of Births, Marriages, and Deaths in Scotland from 1855. Traditionally, researchers had to track down the original records, but for some time now these have been available online in digitized form, which greatly expedites research. Many libraries and archives have research facilities that give access to the above records, as does the website **www.scotlandspeople.gov.uk**.

With luck, these basic sources should bring most researchers some idea of their genealogy back to the eighteenth century, if not further. But there are problems to overcome. The census records should provide reliable information as early as 1841 and could take some people back to the eighteenth century, as could the statutory records of death. Beyond these official records, however, the researcher has to depend on church records.

In 1800 the majority of the population belonged to the main Protestant church—the Church of Scotland. There were, however, Presbyterian dissenters apart from the main church—as well as other denominations such as Episcopalians, Methodists, Quakers, and Roman Catholics—who had their own records. Fortunately, the Catholic records are now available online (**www.nrscotland.gov.uk/research/guides/catholic-parish-registers**). There is, however, a substantial body of church records unavailable online, which means that church records will be of limited use for some researchers. The relevant records may well exist—if so, where are they and are they accessible? The section on church records in this book demonstrates that a substantial number of manuscripts and transcriptions of dissenting churches are available.

## SCOTLANDSPEOPLE

Probably the most efficient way to access, use, and understand the major record sources is by use of the website mentioned on page 1, **www.scotlandspeople.gov.uk**, the official Scottish Government site for searching government records and archives. On this website you can apply for copies of official certificates and research family history, biography, local history, and social history. The site provides a thorough introduction to the basic records that are available to researchers—what is available and how to use them. The records include the post-1855 statutory records of birth, marriage, and death; church registers; census returns; valuation rolls; legal records; wills and testaments; and more. On the site, you can search indexes free of charge and use pay-per-view to view and download digital images of the records you find. You can also purchase vouchers, which are good for two years.

You can also gain access to the ScotlandsPeople records in person at the ScotlandsPeople Centre, located in central Edinburgh, with search rooms in General Register House and New Register House, and at several local family history centers. There is a fee to book a search room seat at the ScotlandsPeople Centre, but you can view as many records as you like for no additional charge. For more information about the ScotlandsPeople Centre, visit **www.nrscotland.gov.uk/research/visit-us/scotlandspeople-centre**.

# SURNAMES

In Scotland, the use of surnames seems to have begun in the twelfth century in the wake of Norman-French immigration. In practice, it took many generations for the adoption of the use of surnames by every level of society. Scottish surnames can be categorized into four distinct groups: names of territorial origin, names of occupational origin, names of patronymic origin, and names of descriptive origin. By the twelfth century the urban dwellers and those in the south-east tended to speak a form of English, while rural dwellers generally spoke Gaelic.

The first people to adopt surnames were the land-owning nobility who, for legal reasons, required some method of identification and generally took the names of their property as their surnames. For example, the surname Abernethy is derived from a place of that name in Strathearn and was first used in 1160 AD by Hugh, the lay abbot of the Culdee monastery there. The majority of early surnames based on indigenous place names are of Celtic origin, whereas some from the south-east are of English origin, while some from the Northern Isles are Norse.

Many basic Scottish surnames are based on the occupation of an early ancestor, and as towns grew and occupations became more specialized, the range of surnames increased. Surnames of patronymic origins are quite common, with a son adopting his father's forename as his surname, later adding "son" to form a distinct surname. In Shetland and Orkney, they followed the Scandinavian practice of each generation having a new surname based on the father's forename; if John Gilbert had a son, his surname would be Gilbertson, while a daughter would have the surname Gilbertsdottir. This practice ended with the introduction of statutory records in 1855.

The study of surnames should be a feature of your family history. Without a doubt, the best source on the subject is George Black's *The Surnames of Scotland* (New York, 1946). If you discover a rare surname in the family, you should be able to find its meaning and history in the said book. If you want to know how common or uncommon a surname is, and its distribution in the nineteenth century, then check Archer Software's *British*

*19th Century Surname Atlas* (CD-ROM), which will provide the answers. It contains over 400,000 surnames that appeared in the 1881 census of Great Britain. I tried searching for four relatively uncommon surnames and got the following results—Skea, with 244 examples, all in Angus or Aberdeenshire; Cardno, with 240 examples, all in Aberdeenshire; Brotchie, with 110 examples in Caithness and Edinburgh; and Cargo, with only 19 examples located in Cumbria or Lanarkshire.

## SCOTTISH ARCHIVES AND LIBRARIES

National

**National Records of Scotland** (NRS), HM General Register House, 2 Princes Street, Edinburgh, EH1 3YY; www.nrscotland.gov.uk/. NRS holds Scottish government records from the 12th century to the present, including registers of births, deaths, marriages, divorces, civil partnerships, dissolutions, and adoptions; census enumeration books; court records; church records; valuation rolls; local and private archives; and much more. Research guides describing their records are available at www.nrscotland.gov.uk/research/guides.

**National Library of Scotland** (NLS), George IV Bridge, Edinburgh, EH1 1EW; www.nls.uk/. The National Library of Scotland is not the main location for original records in Scotland but has a wide range of genealogical resources that may interest you.

The **Scottish Archive Network** (SCAN), www.scan.org.uk/, has partnered with the National Archives of Scotland (NAS), the Heritage Lottery Fund (HLF), and the Genealogical Society of Utah (GSU) to provide access to Scotland's archives by providing a single electronic catalog to the holdings of more than 50 Scottish archives, including many of the ones listed below.

**Scottish Catholic Archives**, Columba House, 16 Drummond Place, Edinburgh, EH3 6PL; www.scottishcatholicarchives.org.uk/. The Scottish Catholic Archives preserves and makes available the archives of the post-reformation Catholic Church in Scotland and abroad.

## Local and Regional

**Aberdeenshire Central Library**, Rosemount Viaduct, Aberdeen, AB25 1GW; www.aberdeencity.gov.uk/services/libraries-and-archives/find-my-local-library/central-library

**Aberdeen City and Aberdeenshire Archives**, Old Aberdeen House, Dunbar St., Old Aberdeen, Aberdeen AB24 3UJ; www.aberdeencity.gov.uk/services/libraries-and-archives/aberdeen-city-and-aberdeenshire-archives

**Aberdeen University Library**, Bedford Road, Aberdeen, AB24 3AA; www.abdn.ac.uk/library/

**Angus Archives**, Hunter Library Restenneth, Forfar DD8 2SZ; www.angusalive.scot/local-family-history/

**Argyll and Bute Archives**, Manse Brae Area Office, Lochgilphead, Argyll PA31 8QU; https://liveargyll.co.uk/facility/archives/

**Ayrshire Archives**, Ayrshire Archives HQ, Watson Peat Building, SAC Auchincruive, Ayr KA65HW; www.ayrshirearchives.org.uk/

**North Ayrshire Library**, 39-41 Princes Street, Ardrossan. KA22 8BT; www.north-ayrshire.gov.uk/libraries/

**South Ayrshire Library**, 12 Main Street, Ayr, KA8 8EB; www.south-ayrshire.gov.uk/libraries/

**Scottish Borders Archive and Local History Service**, The Heritage Hub, Kirkstile, Hawick, TD9 0AE; www.liveborders.org.uk/culture/archives/

**Live Borders Library HQ**, St Mary's Mill, Selkirk, TD7 5EW; www.liveborders.org.uk/culture/libraries/our-libraries/

**Caithness Archives,** The Nuclear and Caithness Archives, Wick Airport, Wick, KW1 4QP; www.highlifehighland.com/nucleus-nuclear-caithness-archives/

**Clackmannanshire Archives**, Speirs Centre, Primrose Place, Alloa, FK10 1AD; www.clacks.gov.uk/culture/archives/

**Dumfries and Galloway Archives & Library**, Ewart Library, Catherine Street, Dumfries, DG1 IJB; www.dumgal.gov.uk/article/15308/Local-archives

**East Dunbartonshire Record Office**, 2-4 West High Street, Kirkintilloch, G66 1AD; www.edlc.co.uk/heritage-arts/archives

**West Dunbartonshire Library**, Strathleven Place, Dunbarton, G82 1BD; www.west-dunbarton.gov.uk/libraries/

**Dundee Central Library**, The Wellgate, Dundee, DD1 1DB; www.leisureandculturedundee.com/library

**Dundee City Archives**, 14 City Square, Dundee, DD1 3BY; www.dundeecity.gov.uk/services/archives-&-libraries

**Dundee University Library and Learning Centre**, Perth Road, Dundee, DD1 4HN; www.dundee.ac.uk/library/

**Edinburgh Central Library**, George IV Bridge, Edinburgh, EH1 1EG; www.edinburgh.gov.uk/centrallibrary

**Edinburgh City Archives**, 253 High Street, Edinburgh, EH1 1YJ; www.edinburgh.gov.uk/archives/edinburgh-city-archives-1/3

**Edinburgh University Library**, George Square, Edinburgh, EH8 9LJ; www.ed.ac.uk/information-services/library-museum-gallery

**Heriot Watt University Library**, Riccarton, Edinburgh, EH14 4AS; www.hw.ac.uk/uk/edinburgh/facilities.htm

**Falkirk Library**, Hope Street, Falkirk, FK1 5AU; www.falkirkcommunitytrust.org/venues/falkirk-library

**Fife Archives**, ON at Fife Collections Centre, Bankhead Central, Bankhead Park, Glenrothes, Fife, KY7 6GH; http://onfife.com/libraries-archives/archives/

**Glasgow City Archives**, The Mitchell Library, North Street, Glasgow, G3 7DN; www.glasgowlife.org.uk/libraries/city-archives

**Glasgow University Archives**, Hillhead Street, Glasgow, G12 8QE; www.gla.ac.uk/myglasgow/archives/

**Highland Archive Centre**, Bught Road, Inverness, IV3 5SS; www.highlifehighland.com/highland-archive-centre/

**North Highland Archive**, The Nuclear and Caithness Archives, Wick Airport, Wick, KW1 4QP; www.highlifehighland.com/nucleus-nuclear-caithness-archives/

**Moray Local Heritage Centre and Archives**, Elgin Library, Cooper Park, Elgin, IV30 1HS; www.moray.gov.uk/moray_standard/page_1537.html

**Orkney Library and Archives**, 44 Junction Road, Kirkwall, KW15 1AG; www.orkneylibrary.org.uk/

**Perth and Kinross Archive**, A K Bell Library, York Place, Perth, PH2 8EP; www.culturepk.org.uk/archive-local-family-history/

**Shetland Library**, Lower Hillhead, Lerwick, ZE1 0EL; www.shetland-library.gov.uk/

**Shetland Museum and Archives**, Hay's Dock, Lerwick, ZE1 0WP; www.shetlandmuseumandarchives.org.uk/

**St. Andrews University Library**, North Street, St. Andrews, KY16 9TR; www.st-andrews.ac.uk/library/

**Stirling Council Archives**, 5 Borrowmeadow Road, Springkerse Industrial Estate, Stirling, FK7 7UW; www.stirlingarchives.scot/

**University of Stirling Library**, Stirling, FK9 4LA; www.stir.ac.uk/about/professional-services/information-services-and-library/

**Stornaway Library**, 19 Cromwell Street, Stornaway, HS1 2DA; www.cne-siar.gov.uk/leisure-sport-and-culture/libraries-and-archives/leabharlannan-nan-eilean-siar/your-library/stornoway-library/

**University of Strathclyde Library**, 101 St James Road, Glasgow, G4 0NS; www.strath.ac.uk/professionalservices/library/visit/

# OTHER USEFUL WEBSITES

**FamilySearch,** www.familysearch.org, makes numerous Scottish records accessible online at no charge, including births and baptisms, church records, Kirk Session records, and marriage records. Details on available Scottish records are available at www.familysearch.org/wiki/en/Scotland_Genealogy.

**GENUKI,** www.genuki.org.uk/big/sct, is a non-commercial service providing links to every imaginable resource related to U.K. and Ireland genealogy.

**Findmypast**, www.findmypast.com, is a subscription service with over 4 billion searchable records.

**Ancestry,** www.ancestry.com, is another subscription site with numerous Scottish records, including census, vital, parish, military, and immigration records, and more.

# Chapter 2

# MAJOR RECORD SOURCES

## POST 1854 STATUTORY REGISTRATION OF BIRTHS, MARRIAGES, DEATHS, DIVORCES, CIVIL PARTNERSHIPS, AND SAME-SEX MARRIAGES

Statutory registration of births, marriages, and deaths in Scotland began 1855. These records are held at the New Register House in Edinburgh and may be consulted in digitized form at the ScotlandsPeople Centre in Edinburgh or online at **www.scotlandspeople.gov.uk**. Also available are divorce records from 1984, civil partnerships from 2005, and same-sex marriages from 2014. Births over 100 years old, marriages over 75 years old, and deaths over 50 years old are restricted. You can order birth, death, marriage, civil partnership, divorce, and dissolution of civil partnership certificates online at **www.scotlandspeople.gov.uk/certificate-search**.

### Birth Records

Researchers will find a great deal of detailed information in the Statutory Register of Births. Most birth records include the name of the child; the date, time, and place of birth; the child's sex; name and occupation of the father; name and maiden surname of the mother; date and place of the parents' marriage; the signature, address, and relation of the informant; and the signature of the registrar. Records for 1855 only contain information about the parents' other children, as well as the ages and birthplaces of the parents.

## Marriage Records

Scottish marriage certificates also provide the researcher with much useful information—the names and addresses of the bride and groom, their occupations, their ages, their status (single, widow, widower, divorced), their places of birth, the names and occupations of their parents, and the name of the minister or priest.

One key piece of information supplied on marriage certificates reveals the religious denomination of the participants by recording which church they belonged to. It is likely that the couple were both of the same denomination, though it is possible that it was a "mixed marriage." Most people in Scotland were likely to be Protestant, probably members of the Church of Scotland, the main Presbyterian church, but there were other Presbyterian churches there as well. Assuming those married were of the Church of Scotland (the Kirk), then the next step would be to consult the Old Parish Registers of baptism and marriage. Couples did not have to be married in church to be legally married. However, both the church and state encouraged "regular" marriages, with banns, and exchange of consent in church before the congregation, and not "penny weddings."

## Death Records

Death records contain information of great value to researchers. Most include the deceased's name; occupation; marital status (and name of spouse, if married); date and place of death; sex; age; and cause of death. Also included are the name and occupation of the deceased's father; the name and maiden surname of the mother; whether the parents are deceased; the signature, address, and relationship of informant; where and when the death was registered; and the signature of the registrar.

The 1855 records only include the names and ages of all children of the deceased (whether living or dead); the place of burial and the undertaker used; the deceased's date and place of birth; and the length of time the deceased had lived in the district. Records from 1965 onward include the occupation of the spouse or civil partner and the mother of the deceased.

Other good sources of death information include obituaries and burial registers, including Frances McDonnell's *Aberdeen Obituaries from 1800 to 1854*, three parts (St. Andrews, 1996, 1997); Edinburgh City Archives' *Greyfriars Church Burial Records 1771-1864* (ECA.SL92); and Perth and Kinross Archives' Perth Burgh Burial Register, 1794-1855 (PKA. PE1.20), which contains full names, ages, date of deaths and burials, names of kin, occupation, details of burial, and name of cemetery.

## Divorce Records

The Statutory Register of Divorces starts on May 1, 1984. The amount of information on a divorce decree is limited. It usually contains the names and addresses of both parties; the Sheriff Court and court reference number; the date and place of marriage; and the date of the divorce decree.

Divorce has been possible in Scotland since 1560. Between 1684 and 1830 there were 904 divorce actions, of which 757 were successful and the rest abandoned or dismissed; 803 were for adultery and 101 for desertion. Before 1770 there was only one or two divorce cases on average, but thereafter there was a marked rise in their number. By 1820 there were roughly 200 cases per year. Legal separations were less common, amounting to 175 between 1700 and 1830.

There are a few books and articles on the subject that are useful to the family historian. Francis J. Grant's *The Commissariat of Edinburgh: Consistorial Processes and Decreets, 1658-1800* (Edinburgh, 1909) largely consists of records of divorce.

A more recent publication is Leah Leneman's *Alienated Affections: The Scottish Experience of Divorce and Separation, 1684-1830* (Edinburgh, 1998), which explores a wide range of divorces in detail, listing about 700 pursuers and defenders, including the following:

> Donald McNair, in Rosemarkie, married Isobel Forbes
> in Edinburgh in 1766, in 1779 she entered a second
> marriage with George Murdoch a porter in Leith in 1779,
> a divorce action in 1789 (NRS.CC8.5.19).
>
> Agnes Kennedy, wife of Andrew Crauford of
> Craufordstone, eloped with Simeon Bardou, a Frenchman

and a soldier in a regiment of dragoons, a divorce action in 1719 (NRS.CC8.6.7).

## CENSUS RECORDS

Scottish censuses have been taken every ten years since 1801, but only since 1841 do the census returns provide useful genealogical data. The returns are closed for 100 years to protect privacy; therefore, the censuses available to researchers at the time of this writing date from 1841 to 1911, inclusive. These have been digitized and are available at the ScotlandsPeople Centre, online at **www.scotlandspeople.gov.uk**, and at local family history centers. The FreeCen census project (**www.freecen. org.uk**), begun in 1999, is in the process of having the 1841, 1851, 1861, 1871, and 1891 censuses transcribed by volunteers, with the goal of providing free internet searches of the nineteenth-century UK census returns. Subscription services Ancestry and Findmypast contain a searchable index, with transcripts of Scottish census records up to 1901. The next census to be released to the public will be the 1921 census, which will become available in 2021.

Census records are particularly useful as they can, on occasion, provide leads back to the mid-eighteenth century. The censuses between 1841 and 1911 provide the following information—full name and address, relationship to the head of household, whether married or single, age, sex, occupation, and place of birth. As there would have been some people in Scotland at the time of the 1841 census aged 70 years or more, it is quite possible to identify ancestors born before 1770. In the 1841 census, the letters E (signifying England & Wales), I (Ireland), or F (foreign) are used for those born outside of Scotland, but in later censuses the exact place of birth—parish, town, and county—is usually shown.

## OLD PARISH REGISTERS OF THE CHURCH OF SCOTLAND, 1553 TO 1854

The major sources of birth, marriage, and death information before 1855 are the baptismal and marriage registers of the Church of Scotland, known as the Old Parish Registers (OPRs). These can be consulted in digitized form at the ScotlandsPeople Centre, online at **www.scotlands people.gov.uk**, and at local family history centers. The OPRs contain data for over 900 Scottish parishes of the Church of Scotland, dating back to the middle of the sixteenth century on a few occasions. The oldest parish record is that listing baptisms and banns of the parish of Errol, dating from 1553. Lowland parish registers generally predate those of Highland parishes.

A few parish registers have been published, including that of Durness, in the far north of Scotland, from 1764 to 1814 (Hew Morrison, Edinburgh, 1911) for a period when Gaelic was the common tongue there. Among the entries is the following:

> Angus Mackay Down Macrobmacrob, a pensioner, also
> lately come from America, and Ann 24 December 1785.
> (Angus was presumably a former soldier who has returned
> from serving during the American War of Independence.)

*The Register of Baptisms, Proclamations, Marriages, and Mortcloth Dues, of the Parish of Torpichen, from 1673 to 1714*, by John MacLeod (Edinburgh, 1911), provides data on families in a parish of Linlithgowshire alias West Lothian. Based on the Kirk Session Records, it includes entries of Mortcloth Dues from 1673 to 1704 (a mortcloth being a shroud used to cover the coffin prior to burial) and provides records of burial, including the following:

> Hugo, son of Hugo Potter, on 2 August 1686, or
> John Gardiner, a tailor in Torpichen, on 25 January
> 1689. (See the Scottish Record Society website, www.
> scottishrecordsociety.org.uk/.)

OPRs are far from comprehensive. Record keeping varied from parish to parish and sometimes not much information was included. Some registers are illegible; others were lost or destroyed. What sources are available when the above church records prove to be non-comprehensive? The next chapter will identify other church and religious sources that are available and where they are located.

# ROMAN CATHOLIC PARISH REGISTERS

The earliest Catholic parish records in Scotland date from 1703 for the mission of Braemar, but the majority date from the nineteenth century. All pre-1855 records–before the introduction of civil registration—and some post-1855 records have been digitized and indexed, and are available at ScotlandsPeople, **www.scotlandspeople.gov.uk**. Catholic Parish Registers mainly consist of baptisms and marriages, though they may also list confirmations, deaths and burials, communicants, sick calls, status animarum, converts, first confessions, and seat rents.

The Scottish Catholic Archives are in two sites, one in Edinburgh and the other in Aberdeen. Aberdeen University library (**www.abdn.ac.uk/special-collections/scottish-catholic-archives-73.php**) contains the historical records dating from before 1800, while the later records are in Columba House, Edinburgh (**www.scottishcatholicarchives.org.uk/**).

Like the OPRs, the comprehensiveness and reliability of the record-keeping in the Catholic registers varied from parish to parish. See the next chapter, Church and Other Religious Records, for more information about the Catholic Church in Scotland, plus a list of relevant publications and archival material.

Chapter 3

# CHURCH AND OTHER RELIGIOUS RECORDS

The Presbyterian Church of Scotland, also known by its Scots language name, the Kirk, is the national church of Scotland. There were several Presbyterian churches that broke away from the Church of Scotland, mainly in the eighteenth and early nineteenth centuries. These have largely returned to the Church of Scotland. Such churches include the Reformed Presbyterian Church, the Original Secession Church, the Associate Synod of the various burgher churches, the Relief Church, the United Secession Church, the United Presbyterian Church, and the Free Church. In 1733 the issue of patronage, whereby the minister was imposed on the congregation, led to the secession of a number of these churches from the Church of Scotland, and the formation of the Secession churches and of the Associate Presbytery. A further secession in 1752 created the Relief Church. This argument over principle within the Presbyterian churches eventually led to a major split in 1843, when around a third of the ministers and congregations of the Kirk left the Church of Scotland to form the Free Church of Scotland. In 1847 the main Secession churches merged to form the United Presbyterian Church. Then the Free Church and the United Presbyterian Church merged in 1900 to form the United Free Church. In 1929 the Church of Scotland and the United Free Church amalgamated.

While the surviving baptismal and marriage registers of the Church of Scotland are commonly available on microfiche, microfilm, and in digitized version online, as described in the previous chapter, they are not comprehensive, and the records of the other Presbyterian churches are not always so readily available. Some records of the other Presbyterian churches exist in their original form in the churches or in libraries and archives throughout Scotland. But in many cases they are not easily accessible. This chapter, therefore, concentrates on publications, manuscripts, and other unpublished sources of the various Presbyterian churches and other religious groups, such as the Society of Friends (Quakers) and the Jews. If you are fortunate, the publications you wish to consult will have been digitized and made viewable online on sites such as HathiTrust (**www.hathitrust.org/**).

The registers of the Free Church and other dissenting churches are gradually being made available on the ScotlandsPeople website (**www.scotlandspeople.gov.uk**), and in the meantime can be found in the National Records of Scotland or in local archives. Entries from the Registers of some Free and other Dissenting Churches have been transcribed and published.

## CHURCH OF SCOTLAND

As stated in the previous chapter, Church of Scotland parish registers are available online at **www.scotlandspeople.gov.uk**, but they are not comprehensive. Below are publications that will help fill in the gaps. Particularly useful is *Fasti Ecclesiae Scoticanae* (Hew Scott and others, 10 volumes, Edinburgh, 1915-1981), a major source of biographical data on the ministers of the Church of Scotland and their families, organized by presbytery and then by parish. For example,

> John Guthrie, born 13 August 1631, son of Reverend
> James Guthrie in Arbirlot, Angus, was minister of the
> Second Charge of Dundee from 1667 to 1685. He
> married an Isobel Lamb, and they were parents of John,
> Isobel, James, Nicolas, Robert, Ann and Alexander
> *(Fasti.5.320).*

***Publications.*** The earliest surviving presbytery records in Scotland are found in *Stirling Presbytery Records, from 1581 to 1587* (James Kirk, Edinburgh, 1981).

*Records of the Presbyteries of Inverness and Dingwall, 1643-1688* (W. Mackay, Edinburgh, 1896) lists local men brought before the presbytery accused of participating in the Duke of Hamilton's invasion of England in support of Charles II in 1648 (see pages 154–160, also 367–370). The same source has a list of elders and deacons of the parish of Wardlaw, also those of Daviot and Dunlechety, dated May 1682 (see pages 106–108).

Other publications include *The Kirks of Edinburgh, 1560-1984, Congregations, Churches and Ministers of the Presbytery of Edinburgh Church of Scotland* (A. I. Dunlop, Edinburgh, 1988); *Scottish Parish Clergy at the Reformation, 1540-1574* (Charles H. Haws, Edinburgh, 1972); *The Divinity Professors in the University of Glasgow from 1640 to 1903* (H. M. B. Reid, Glasgow, 1923); *The Kirks of Dundee Presbytery, 1558-1999* (Ian McCraw, Dundee, 2000); *The Face of Christ in Dundee, 1000 to 2000 AD* (A. J. Ferrie, Dundee, 2000); *Reformation, Dissent and Diversity, the Story of Scotland's Churches, from 1560 to 1960* (Andrew Muirhead, London, 2015).

## KIRK SESSION RECORDS

A feature of the Church of Scotland and other Presbyterian churches is the Kirk Session, which is the lowest court of the church. This is formed by the parish minister and the elders of the congregation. Its function is to maintain order, thus acting as an agent of social control. Kirk Session Records are invaluable for family history research. Parishioners were brought before the local Kirk Session for various reasons—for example, practicing archery or golfing rather than attending church. Probably the most useful data recorded in the records pertains to illegitimacy. Unless the man responsible was identified and persuaded to marry or financially support the child, the cost of maintaining the child would fall on the parish. The Kirk Session was also responsible for raising money to support the poor and needy.

Some minutes of the Kirk Sessions have survived from the late sixteenth century, but they are more likely available from the seventeenth century. They can be consulted at the National Records of Scotland, though some have been returned to local archives. Edinburgh Kirk Session Records from 1573 to 1882 are in the Edinburgh City Archives, and Alva Kirk Session Records from 1666 to 1984 are in the Stirling Archives. The National Records of Scotland has begun releasing church court records for access online on the ScotlandsPeople website (**www.scotlandspeople.gov.uk/**). As of this writing, baptism, marriage, and burial registers from Kirk Session Records for congregations of the Reformed Presbyterian Church, Original Secession Church (and subsequent Secession churches), the Relief Church, and the Free Church have been made available.

***Publications.*** One of the few Kirk Session Records to have been published are those of Galston from 1568 to 1595 (Margaret Sanderson, Edinburgh, 2019), which include baptisms and marriages. Another publication dealing with Kirk Session Records is *The Register of the Kirk Session of St. Andrews, 1559-1600*, transcribed by D. H. Fleming and published by the Scottish History Society in Edinburgh in 1890. The following excerpt is not untypical of much of the activities of the Kirk Sessions of that period:

> Wednesday the xvj of Januar, 1600….The quhilk day,
> Jonet Cluny, now in this citie fugitive fra the discipline
> of the kirk of Forgund in Fyiff, being callit comperit, and
> being accusit fornication with Alexander Bruce, son to
> Robert Bruce of Pitlethy; and confest carnall copulation
> with Dauid Dury hir maister, quhilk wes adultrie; and
> thairfoir is remittit to the discipline of Forgund kirk, the
> adulterie being committit in that parrochin.

# FREE CHURCH

In 1843 there occurred what is known as the Disruption of the Church of Scotland, when around one-third of the ministers and congregations left the Church of Scotland on a matter of principle. The outcome was initially the formation of the Free Church of Scotland, and later the

United Presbyterian Church of Scotland and other smaller denominations. Eventually, most of these denominations merged and reunited with the Church of Scotland. The Church of Scotland was formed at the Reformation and was the "Established Church"; those churches that left the Established Church in 1843 were known as "Free Churches."

**Publications.** Publications concerning the Free Church include *The Annals of the Free Church of Scotland, 1843-1900*, 2 vols. (W. Ewing, Edinburgh, 1914), which provides an insight into the origins, development, and accessions to the Free Church of Scotland of the Old Light Burghers, the United Original Seceders, and the Reformed Presbyterians, as well as biographical data on the professors of the Church and the ordained ministers and missionaries.

Published sources listing baptisms and marriages include *Lochee West United Free Church, 1826-1926* (H. Williamson, Dundee, 1927); *Dalkeith Free Church baptisms, 1843-1854 & Marriages for 1848* (R.W. Cockburn, Scottish Genealogy Society, 2012–these are online at Findmypast.com in the Scotland, Edinburgh & Lothian Birth & Baptism Index; *Edinburgh, South College Relief Church: baptismal records, 1766-1783)* (R.W. Cockburn, Scottish Genealogy Society, 2011); *Lady Glenorchy Free Church: baptisms, 1843-1856* (D.R. Torrance, Scottish Genealogy Society, 2001); *Kirkhill Free Church Births and Baptisms, 1843-1854* (S. Farrell, Inverness, 2013); *Kirlarlity Free Church Births and Baptisms, 1843-1854* (S. Farrell, Inverness, 2013); *Inverness East Free Church baptisms 1843-1858* (S. Farrell, Inverness, 2012); *Inverness, Queen Street, United Presbyterian Church Baptisms, 1839-1854, and 1860-1871* (S. Farrell, Inverness, 2013); *Botriphnie Free Church Baptisms 1843-1869* (S. Farrell, Moray, 2019); *Strachan Free Church Baptisms 1836-1924* (S. Farrell, Edinburgh, 2017; *Watten Free Church, Births and Baptisms, 1844-1873* (S. Farrell, Inverness, 2016); *Pultneytown Free Church, Births and Baptisms, 1845-1854* (S. Farrell, Inverness, 2016); *Dunnet Free Church, Births/Baptisms, 1843-1867* (S. Farrell, Inverness, 2014); *Huntly Free Church, Births and Baptisms, 1839-1853* (S. Farrell, Edinburgh, 2017); *Canisbay Free Church Births and Baptisms, 1843-1875* (S. Farrell, Inverness, 2014); *Thurso Free Church, Births and Baptisms, 1843-1854* (S. Farrell, Inverness, 2018); *Bruan Free*

*Church, Births and Baptisms, 1847-1906* (S. Farrell, Inverness, 2015); *Lybster Free Church, births and baptisms, 1843-1875* (S. Farrell, Inverness, 2015); *Creich Free Church, Births and Baptisms, 1843-1897* (S. Farrell, Inverness, 2013); *Knockbain Free Church Births and Baptisms, 1843-1854* (S. Farrell, Inverness, 2012); *Killearnan Free Church Baptisms 1843-1851* (S. Farrell, Inverness, 2012); *Tongue Free Church Baptisms, 1843-1887* (S. Farrell, Inverness, 2013); *Durness Free Church, Baptisms 1843-1919* (S. Farrell, Inverness, 2013); *Alness Free Church, Baptisms 1843-1929* (S. Farrell, Inverness, 2011); *Rogart Free Church, Births and Baptisms, 1843-1854, also 1873-1896* (S. Farrell, Inverness, 2013); *Lairg Free Church Births and Baptisms 1844-1854* (S. Farrell, Inverness, 2013); *Resolis Free Church, Baptisms 1843-1868* (S. Farrell, Inverness, 2012); *Fortrose Free Church Baptisms, 1844-1855* (S. Farrell, Inverness, 2012); *Wick Free Church, births and baptisms, 1845-1860* (S. Farrell, Inverness, 2017); *Fearn Free Church, Baptisms, 1844-1890* (S. Farrell, Inverness, 2011); *Tain Free Church, 1843-1866* (S. Farrell, Inverness, 2012); *Kinloss and Findhorn, Free Church, Births and Baptisms, 1843-1856* (S. Farrell, Moray, 2014*)*; *Edderton Free Church, Baptisms 1847-1865* (S. Farrell, Inverness, 2012); *Burghead Free Church Baptisms, 1850-1854* (D. Stewart, Moray, 2010); and *The Free Church of Scotland, 1843-1910* (A.M. Stewart).

**Records in Archives.** The Free Churches remained Presbyterian in structure and maintained the same records for baptisms, marriages, and Kirk Session Records. Records of baptisms from many Free Churches are available at National Records of Scotland.

St. Andrews University Library, Special Collections, has the following records: Anstruther Free Church, Baptisms (SAUL.CH3.1560/4.D.5); Auchter-muchty Free Church, Baptisms, 1843-1921 (SAUL.CH3.604.8.4.E.5); Creich and Flisk, Free Church, Baptisms, 1843-1886 (SAUL.CH3.1582.4.C.1); Grangemouth, Baptisms, 1839-1843 (SAUL.CH3.1582.4.C.1); and Flisk and Creich, Baptisms, 1843-1886 (SAUL.CH3.1.1582/4/C/1).

Shetland Free Church records are in the Shetland Archives (SA.CH3).

# ASSOCIATE CHURCH

The Church of Scotland experienced several schisms during the eighteenth century, usually on matters of principle. In 1733 several ministers, often called "seceders," withdrew from the Kirk when only the heritors and the elders were given the right to nominate ministers, and they formed the Associate Presbytery. By 1745 the Presbytery had grown and was reorganized into the Associate Synod. In 1747 this church split over the issue of the Burgher Oath, which required holders of public offices to take an oath affirming the religion "presently professed in this kingdom." The Burghers—those that supported the oath—called themselves the Associate Synod, while the Anti-Burghers—those who were against the oath—became the General Associate Synod. By the end of the century, both divisions further split apart over questions of civil magistracy into Old-Light Anti-Burghers and New-Light Anti-Burghers, and Old-Light Burghers and New-Light Burghers. In 1820 the New-Light Burghers and the New-Light Anti-Burghers united to form the United Secession Church.

***Publications.*** Publications containing baptisms and marriages include *Montrose Associate Church Baptisms, 1743-1831* (S. Farrell, Edinburgh, 2019); *Broughton Place Associate Congregation, Edinburgh: Names of Members, 1795 & Baptisms, 1836-1839* (Russell W. Cockburn, Edinburgh, 2013); *The Baptismal Diary of the Reverend William Inglis of Dumfries* (Ian A. McClumpha and Alison Etchells, Edinburgh, 2003), which contains baptisms in the Associate Congregations in Dumfries from 1765 to 1826, also marriages in the parish of Urr from 1817 to 1841; *Nigg Associate Presbyterian Church, Births and Baptisms, 1765-1867, and Marriages c1800-1866* (S. Farrell, Inverness. 2014).

***Records in Archives and Libraries.*** St. Andrews University Library, Special Collections, has Ceres Associate Congregation, baptisms, 1738-1891 (SAUL.CH3.54.10-12); Crail Associate Congregation, baptisms, 1821-1852 (SAUL.CH3.1562.1.4.D.7); Newburgh Associate Congregation, baptisms, 1785, 1821-1864 (SAUL.CH3.242.1.4.E.4); Rathillet Burgher Church, baptisms, 1781-1884 (SAUL.CH3.1565/4.C.2); and St. Andrews, Burgher Church, baptisms, 1829-1934 (SAUL.CH3.1584.4.C.4).

The National Records of Scotland has Alyth Associate Secession Records, 1781-1927 (NRS.CH3.15), as well as records of the Dunblane Associate Church from 1784-1817 (NRS.CH3).

Anti-Burgher church records are, to some extent, in the National Records of Scotland. Examples are Edinburgh Associate Presbytery from 1744 (NRS.CH3/111); Elgin Anti-Burgher Presbytery from 1770 (NRS. CH3,121); Forfar Anti-Burgher Presbytery from 1788 (NRS.CH3.133); and Perth Anti-Burgher Presbytery from 1784 (NRS.CH3.260). Others may be found in regional archives of libraries; for example, Borders Archives has the Records of Earlston and Kelso Anti-Burgher Presbytery. St. Andrews University Library has Rathillet Burgher Church, baptisms, 1781-1884 (SAUL.CH3.1565/4.C.2); and St. Andrews, Burgher Church, baptisms, 1829-1934 (SAUL.CH3.1584.4.C.4).

## THE RELIEF CHURCH

The Relief Church dates from 1752 when Thomas Gillespie was deposed from the Church of Scotland for defending the congregation's sole right to choose its minister. Eventually, the Relief Church had 60 congregations and 36.000 members. In 1847 it merged with the United Secession Church to form the United Presbyterian Church of Scotland.

## THE UNITED PRESBYTERIAN CHURCH

Old-Light Burghers, New-Light Burghers, Old-Light Anti-Burghers, and New-Light Anti-Burghers (see above description of the Associate Church) reunited and in 1847 joined the United Presbyterian Church.

**Publications.** The *History of the Congregations of the United Presbyterian Church, 1733-1900* (Robert Small, Edinburgh, 1904) not only provides detailed information on the presbyteries and congregations of the church but also contains lists of ministers and others prominent in the church. The following is an example of the content:

> John Cleland, formerly a schoolmaster in
> Cambuskenneth, entered the Associate Presbytery in

March 1739, then followed Balfron in the Presbytery of
Dunbarton on 8 June 1742, at the Breach of 1747 he
went to the Anti-burgher side and took the bulk of his
people with him. In 1752 the congregation divided and
on 1 May 1752 he was transferred with them.

Other publications include *Balgedie, United Presbyterian Church,
Kinross-shire, baptisms, 1829-1922* (S. Farrell, Edinburgh, 2017); and
*Aberdeen Charlotte Street, United Presbyterian Church Baptisms, 1845-
1855 & 1868-1903* (S. Farrell, Edinburgh, 2016).

# METHODIST CHURCH

Methodism was brought to Scotland by John Wesley in 1751. The
church records are mainly held in the National Records of Scotland
and are generally from the nineteenth century.

*Publications.* Scottish Methodism in the Early Victorian Period (Jabez
Bunting, A. J. Hayes and D. A. Bowland, Edinburgh, 1976); *The
Wesleyan Register of Baptisms, Dundee 1785-1898* (D. Firth, Dundee,
2000); *Inverness Methodist Church Baptisms, 1836-1914* (S Farrell, Inverness, 2016); *Methodism in Scotland* (W. F. Swift, 1974).

*Records in Archives.* Examples of records held by the National Records of Scotland are Edinburgh District Wesleyan Methodist Circuit
1806-1979—for example, Nicolson Square baptisms from 1801 to
1871 (NRS.CH11.2.14); Sinclairtown, Kirkcaldy, from 1883; Dunbar, 1835-2016, baptisms 1814-1884 (NRS.CH11.6.7); Easter Road,
Leith, baptismal Chapel, 1834-1875 (NRS.CH11.12.14); Dalkeith,
baptisms, 1855-1914 (NRS.CH11.17.6); Leith, Great Junction Street,
baptisms, 1834-1875 (NRS.CH11.12.14); Motherwell, baptisms,
1856-1914 (NRS.CH11.31.11-13); and Ayr, baptisms, 1826-1906
(NRS.CH11.59.5).

Glasgow City Archives has some Methodist records for Glasgow and
for Lanarkshire, mostly after 1850 (GCA.TD853) The first Methodist
church in Dundee was opened in 1778. Dundee City Archives has
records of Peter Street Chapel and Victoria Road Church, with baptis-

mal registers from 1785 to 1898 (DCA.GD.MC.126). Aberdeen City Archives holds the records of many of the Methodist churches in the North of Scotland circuit—for example, for Cullen (ACA.PD14.1-11), Portlessie (ACA.PD1), and Peterhead (ACA.PD62). Stirling Archives has the Stirling and Doune Circuit of the Wesleyan Church records from 1842 and 1999; Shetland Archives has the records of the local Free Churches (ZA.CH3).

## SECESSION CHURCH

The Original Secession Church dates from 14 March 1744 when twenty ministers withdrew from the Church of Scotland, claiming that it was no longer following the aims of the Covenanters (see page 96) of the mid-seventeenth century. The Secession Church was Calvinistic, Presbyterian, and more evangelical than the Established Church of Scotland.

*Publications.* *Registers of the Secession Churches in Scotland* (Diane Baptie, Edinburgh, 2000) states that most records of baptisms and marriages of the Secession churches are found in the Kirk Session Minutes, which are generally held in the National Records of Scotland in Edinburgh. The book identifies the archives containing Secession Church data and contains a comprehensive list of all the Secession Church records containing baptisms and marriages that are held in the NRS.

In 1900 most Secession churches merged to form the United Free Kirk, which merged with the Church of Scotland in 1929. See *Annals and Statistics of the Original Session Church* (David Scott, Edinburgh, 1886), which contains lists of divinity students, probationers, and ministers from 1742, with biographical data; for example,

> David Simpson from Boardmills in Ireland, educated at
> Divinity Hall, licensed by the Presbytery of Down on 6
> November 1849, ordained at Brechin on 1 January 1851,
> united with the Free Church of Scotland in 1852, translated
> to Laurencekirk on 29 June 1854.

*Records in Archives.* Secession Church records held in the NRS in Edinburgh include those of Kilmarnock Crookedholm, baptisms from 1802 to 1837 (NRS.CH3.1318.1); a list of members and adherents in 1802 (NRS.CH3.1318.4); and adherents rolls 1840 to 1860, 1872 to 1910 (NRS.CH3.1318.25).

# CONGREGATIONAL CHURCH

The Congregational Church originated in England in the early seventeenth century. It operated in some parts of Scotland during the Cromwellian period, then declined until the revival of Scottish Congregationalism, which was derived from the work of Robert and James Haldane in the late eighteenth century. The Scottish Congregational Union was founded in 1812.

**Publications.** *The Membership Roll of Frederick Street, Aberdeen, Congregational Chapel, 1807-1859* (Ronald Leith, Aberdeen, 1986); *Two Hundred Years of Congregationalism in Dundee 1795-1995* (Dundee, 1995); *The Scottish Congregational Ministry, 1794-1993* (W. D. McNaughton, Glasgow, 1993); *A History of Scottish Congregationalism* (H. Escott, Edinburgh, 1960); *A History of Congregational Independency in Scotland* (James Ross, Glasgow, 1900); *Biographical Sketches of Early Scottish Congregational Ministers, from 1798 to 1851* (Robert Kinniburgh, Edinburgh, 1851).

**Records in Archives.** Congregational Church records in the NRS include Glasgow, Elgin Place, roll of members 1835-1962 (NRS.CH14.2.1); Dundee Ward Chapel, communicant's roll books, pre-1848 to 1938 (NRS.CH14.4.34-36; NRS.276.150); Edinburgh Augustine Church, communion rolls, 1833-1886 (NRS.CH14.14.43-46); Brighton Street, Edinburgh, baptismal register, 1876-1907 (NRS.CH14.18.6); Richmond Place, Edinburgh, Roll of Members 1831-1903 (NRS.CH14.19.1). Fife Archives has the records of the Congregational Church in Kirkcaldy, from 1803 to 2002 (FA.A.ACB).

Dundee City Archives has the records of Ward Chapel Congregational Church, Dundee (186 items; DCA.CH14/4), including membership rolls and admissions 1848-1864 and an index to baptisms 1853-1855 (DCA.CH14.4.59-60); Panmure Street Chapel, membership rolls,

1853-1890 (DCA.CH14.12.18-20); Panmure Trinity Congregational-ist Church, Dundee, 1839-1984 (45 items), including membership rolls, 1853-1960; Arbroath Congregational Church, established in 1799, list of members c1850-1967 (DCA.GD.CU.ARB. 5/1-4); miscellaneous records such as "a certificate confirming the admission of Elizabeth Nicol, wife of Lewis Nicol, into the membership of the First Presbyterian Church of Springfield, Massachusetts, 12 August 1895" (DCA.GD.CU. ARB.11.4; NRAS.2994); Broughty Ferry Congregational Church, membership roll, 1864-1922 (DCA.GD.BF.CU.4.1); and Princes Street Congregational Church, 1839 (DCA.GD.CU.D.PS).

Glasgow City Archives has various local Congregational Church records from the mid-nineteenth century, but no baptisms (GCA.TD1332). Dalkeith Burgher Congregational Church has baptisms from 1747 to 1763. Aberdeen City Archives has local Congregational Church records (ACA.CC1-18).

## BAPTIST CHURCH

Baptists first appeared in Scotland during the Cromwellian Occupation around 1651, but it was not until 1769 that it became established in widely dispersed locations such as Caithness and Edinburgh. Most of the various independent Baptist churches in Scotland merged in 1869 to form the Baptist Union in Scotland. The Dundee Baptist Church can be traced back to 1769, with the first location being in Seagait, with the current main Central Baptist Church being located in Ward Road, Dundee.

**Publications.** *The History of the Baptists in Scotland* (G. Yuille, Edinburgh, 1926); *The First Hundred Years of the Baptist Union of Scotland* (Derek Boyd Murray, Glasgow, 1969); *The Baptists in Scotland, a History* (David W. Bebbington, Glasgow, 1968).

**Records in Archives.** Dundee City Archives has records of the Baptist churches in Dundee (DCA.GD.CH.B1/2), including Long Wynd Baptist Church from 1874, Seagait Baptist Church from 1841; Ward Road Baptist Church from 1895; Bell Street Chapel from 1868; Rattray Street from 1769, later Baptist Church in Meadowside membership rolls from 1846, with baptisms, etc.

Glasgow City Archives has some local Baptist Church records, for example those of Paisley from 1798, but no baptisms (GCA.TD1080). Stirling Archives has the Alloa Baptist records from 1879 to 1934.

## UNITARIAN CHURCH

Unitarian churches were founded in Edinburgh in the mid-eighteenth century, and in Dundee, Glasgow, and Montrose later in that century.

***Records in Archives***. Notably, St. Mark's records date from 1755 (NRS. CH15.1). The Dundee City Archives has records for the Unitarian Church, Dundee, from 1783 to 1969, and a baptismal register from 1868 to 1926 (DCA.GD.UC.1.1). Glasgow City Archives has some records of the Unitarian churches in Glasgow. The origin of the church in Glasgow goes back to 1787, with the first chapel being formed on Union Street in 1812 (GCA.TD983). No records of baptisms in Unitarian churches are held in the Glasgow City Archives.

## SCOTTISH EPISCOPAL CHURCH

Initially, in the period after the Reformation of 1560 and under the influence of John Knox, the Church of Scotland followed a Calvinist or Presbyterian form. However, from 1592 to 1688 it was sometimes Episcopalian and at other times Presbyterian. In 1689 King William—unable to persuade the Scots bishops to break their vow—decreed that henceforth the Church of Scotland be Presbyterian. As a result, some ministers and congregations, especially those in North East Scotland, formed the Scottish Episcopal Church. Some Episcopalian ministers were prominent in the colonies, including James Blair (1656-1743), Commissary of Virginia and founder of the College of William and Mary. The Episcopalians were generally supporters of the exiled House of Stuart and the Jacobite cause. Consequently, with the failure of the Jacobites in 1715 and 1745, the Episcopal Church was subject to penal law and could not operate openly until the death of Bonnie Prince Charlie in 1788.

During this period there were two distinct Episcopalian churches in Scotland. One was the Scotch Episcopal Church, which was pro-Jacobite and subject to severe penal laws, and the other was the Qualified Episcopal Church, which prayed for the Hanoverian monarchs, used the English liturgy and prayer book, and employed Anglican clergymen. The Scotch Episcopal Church was found in the North East and the Highlands, while the Qualified Episcopal chapels were in the South East, which reflected a degree of English immigration. Therefore, the registers of the Episcopal Church are far from comprehensive and are scattered throughout churches and archives. A handful have been published, but most are in manuscript form.

After the American Revolution, the Episcopalian Church in America required a bishop. The Church of England was unwilling to consecrate Samuel Seabury, as he would not take an Oath of Allegiance to the King; consequently, Seabury was consecrated by the Scottish Episcopalian bishops in Aberdeen in 1784.

The registers of the Episcopal Church of Scotland have yet to be made available on the ScotlandsPeople website; in the meantime, they can be found in the National Records of Scotland (NRS reference CH12) or in local archives.

**Publications**. *Scots Episcopalians at Home and Abroad, 1689-1800* (David Dobson, Baltimore, 2011) contains listings such as the following:

> Alexander Henderson, born 1737, son of the Reverend
> Richard Henderson in Blantyre, Lanarkshire, was
> educated at the University of Glasgow, emigrated to
> Virginia in 1756, a merchant and tobacco factor in
> Colchester, Occoquan, and Dumfries, a vestryman of
> Pohick church in the parish of Truro, Fairfax County, in
> 1774, died 1815 in Dumfries, Virginia.

Other publications include *Register of Births and Marriages for the Episcopal Congregation at St. Andrews, 1722-1787* (Canon Winter, Edinburgh, 1916); *Dundee Episcopalians, 1715-1815* (David Dobson, Dundee,

2011); *Register of the Episcopal Congregations in Leith from 1733 to 1775* (Angus McIntyre, Edinburgh, 1949); *Scottish Episcopal Clergy, 1689-2000* (David M. Bertie, Edinburgh, 2000); *Register of Baptisms in the Episcopal Churches of Kilmonaveonaig, Strathtay and Strathtummel, Perthshire, 1812-1830* (C. Bowstead, Edinburgh, 1910); *Elgin Episcopal Church Baptisms, 1721-1740, 1780-1855* (S. Farrell, Moray, 2011); *Episcopacy in Forfar, 1560-1910* (R. W. Dill, Forfar, 1911); *A History of the Episcopal Church in the Diocese of Moray* (J. B. Craven, London, 1889); *The Episcopal History of Perth, 1689-1894* (George T. S. Farquhar, Perth, 1884); and *A Short History of the Episcopal Church in Scotland*, Second Edition (Frederick Goldie, Edinburgh, 1976).

*The Diocese and Presbytery of Dunkeld, from 1660 to 1689* (J. Hunter, New York, 1917), is an excellent source, with much detail, covering a period when the Church of Scotland was ruled by bishops. *The Register of the Diocesan Synod of Dunblane, 1662-1683* (J. Wilson, Edinburgh, 1877) provides insight into a neighboring diocese around the same time.

The following is an example of the information in *Ruthven Episcopal Church Baptisms 1762-1779 and 1799-1834* (S. Farrell, Moray, 2011):

> Anne Lobban, born 9 June 1762, baptised 10 June 1762, daughter of James Lobban and his wife Anne Sandeson in Wardieside, sponsors George Lobban and Margaret Geddes.

**Records in Archives.** The NRS contains the manuscript records of several Episcopalian congregations, including Edinburgh, St. Matthew, baptisms 1886-1897 (NRS.CH12.42.1); Biel, St. Margaret, baptisms 1885-1952 (NRS.CH12.45.1); Armadale, St. Paul, baptisms, 1862-1899 (NRS.CH12.46.1); Edinburgh, St. Andrew's, baptisms 1857-1949 (NRS.CH12.48.1-2); Longside, St. John, baptisms 1727-1892 (NRS.CH12.50.1); Cruden, St. James the Less, baptisms, 1807-1861 (NRS.CH12.50.1); Ellon, St. Mary on the Rock, baptisms, 1816-1871 (NRS.CH12.50.2); Meiklefolla and Lottlefolla, baptisms, 1775-1777 (NRS.CH12.50.2); Auchmunrick, 1777, baptisms (NRS.CH12.50.2); Portsoy and Banff, baptisms, 1778 (NRS.CH12.50.2); Tillydesk and Chapelhall, baptisms, 1784-1790, and 1803-1816 (NRS.CH12.50.2);

Banff, St. Andrew, baptisms, 1723-1752 (NRS.CH12.50.3); Cumines-town, St. Luke, baptisms, 1848-1883 (NRS.CH12.50.3); Turriff, St. Congan, baptisms, 1776-1894 (NRS.CH12.50.3); Aberdeen, St. John the Evangelist, baptisms, 1778-1938 (NRS.CH12.50.3); Aberdeen, Cathedral of St. Andrew, baptisms 1817-1878 (NRS.CH12.50.4); Buckie, All Saints, baptisms, 1762-1834 (NRS.CH12.50.5); Edinburgh, Dean Bridge, baptisms, 1878-1914 (NRS.CH12.52.3); Edinburgh, Joppa, baptisms, 1876-1921 (NRS.CH12.58.1); Edinburgh, Brougham Street, baptisms 1859-1920 (NRS.CH12.91.1-6).

**DUNDEE EPISCOPALIANS, 1715-1815**

chant and James Johnston a writer both in Dundee, were godfathers while the godmothers were the wives of David Fotheringham and Ro Man merchant in Dundee. [BN] [ECD]

CRICHTON, ANNA, dau of Thomas Crichton surgeon apothecary Dundee, bapt 5 May 1725, the laird of Monorgan was godfather whi the mother of Mrs Thomas Crichton and Mrs Ogilvy relict of Ogilvy Newhall the younger were godmothers. [BN]

CRICHTON, CLEMENTINA ANN MARGARET, dau of Thoma Crichton surgeon apothecary in Dundee, was bapt 28 November 17 the laird of Monorgan was godfather while Mr Crichton's mother an lady of Dr Fotheringham were godmothers. [BN]

CRICHTON, DAVID, son of Alexander Crichton in the Seagate, w bapt 9 April 1723. [BN]

CRICHTON, ELIZABETH, dau of Thomas Crichton surgeon apot cary in Dundee, was bapt 3 February 1724, the laird of Monorgan wa godfather while Lady Kinloch and Mr Crichton's mother were godmo ers. [BN]

CRICHTON, HENRY, son of Thomas Crichton a surgeon apothecar Dundee, was bapt 7 December 1722, James Kinloch of that Ilk and Henry Crawford laird of Monorgan were godfathers, and lady .... Tho mas Crichton's sister was godmother. [BN]

CRICHTON, PATRICK, son of Patrick Crichton of Crunan, was bap 20 N ... 1705 D ... D ... Dr Kinloch were godfathe

Church list of Dundee Episcopalians *(courtesy of the author, D. Dobson)*

Dundee City Archives has records of St. Paul's Cathedral, Dundee (DCA.GD.EC.DIO) from 1757, including a list of the congregation living in the Nethergait, Dundee, in 1763. St. Andrew's By-the-Green Episcopal Church Baptisms 1800-1854 are available online at **www. glasgowfamilyhistory.org.uk/ExploreRecords/Documents/St Andrews Baptisms by year.pdf.**

Aberdeen City Archives holds the records of a number of Episcopalian churches in Aberdeen and Banffshire, for example St. James, Aberdeen, from 1804 to 2005 (ACA.DD15); St. John's, Aberdeen, from 1706 to 1992 (DD540); St. Andrew's, Banff, baptisms, 1723 to 1752, and marriages, 1723 to 1745 (ACA.DD307.2.1); and Longside Episcopal records, 1727-1850 (AUL.ms3320/39). Aberdeen University Library has Longside Episcopal registers from 1727 to 1850 (AUL.ms.3320.39).

Dundee University Archives has the Brechin Diocesesan Library (DUA. BrMS3/), which contains the parish records of Episcopalian churches in Angus and the Mearns. It also has transcripts: Old Aberdeen baptisms ,1730-1752 (DUA.BrMS3.dc1); Brechin, marriages, births, and deaths (DUA.BrMS.dc2/2) (also see *The Scottish Antiquary*, xiv); Macterry, 1772-1784, Tillydesk and Chapelhall, 1784-1790 (DUA.Br.MS.dc2/4); Old Deer, baptisms, 1681-1834 (DUA.Br.MS.DC3); Drumlithie, baptisms, 1818-1912 (DUA.Br.MS.DC/9.1); Fasque, baptisms, 1849-1919 (DUA. Br.MS.DC/9.2); Arbuthnott, Fettercairn, Fordoun, Glenbervie, Kinneff, Laurencekirk, Montrose, and St. Cyrus, baptisms, 1800-1825 (DUA. Br.MS.DC/10.2); Muchals, etc., baptisms, 1729-1739, 1788-1815 (DUA.Br.MS.DC/11.1); Old St. Paul's, Edinburgh, baptisms, 1735-1765 (DUA.Br.MS.DC/12) (also see *The Scottish Antiquary*, v.146-); Blairgowrie, baptisms, 1712-1718 (DUA.Br.MS.DC/13.1); Blairdaff and Rosehill plus misc. parishes in Mearns and Angus, baptisms, 1729-1769 (DUA.Br.MS. DC/16); Luthermuir, baptisms, 1770-1789 (DUA.Br.MS.DC/16); Laurencekirk, etc., baptisms, 1814-1834 (DUA.DC/16); Lethnot, Lochlee, etc., baptisms, 1723-1735 (DUA.Br.MS.DC/17A); Arbroath, baptisms, 1812-1949 (DUA.Br.MS6.3); Stonehaven, baptisms, 1756-1878 (DUA. Br.MS.9/1/1/2); Muchalls, baptisms, 1727-1881 (DUA.Br.MS.10.1.1.1); Broughty Ferry, baptisms, 1849-1888 (DUA.Br.MS.15.1-2); Brechin, baptisms, 1812-1917 (DUA.Br.ms16/4/1).

Glasgow City Archives has some Episcopalian records, including Christ Church, Glasgow, baptisms from 1859 to 1899 (GCA.TD1378.9/10/ 11/12/13/14); St. Jude's, Glasgow, baptisms from 1838 to 1869 (GCA. TD1378.9.2/3). There are others in the Archives but of later dates.

St. Andrews University Library has Pittenweem Episcopal, baptisms, 1800-1908 (SAUL.msdep127); St. Andrews, Episcopal, baptisms, 1722-1740, 1748-1787, 1823-1861 (SAUL).

Edinburgh City Archives has the records of some Episcopalian churches in the city, which include baptismal, marriage, and burial registers: Old St. Paul's, 1735-1969 (ECA.ED10); St. Mark's in Portobello, 1828-1978 (ECA.SL67); St. Paul and St. George's, 1712-1988 (ECA.ED67); and St. Peter's, 1807-1977 (ECA. Accn.706).

Examples of the information found in Episcopal baptism records are as follows:

> James Aberdeen, son of Alexander Aberdeen, a merchant, was baptised in St. Paul's, Aberdeen, on 22 February 1722. Witnesses were James Brebner and Thomas Shand, merchants in Aberdeen. (St. Paul's, Aberdeen Register of Baptisms), while elsewhere in Aberdeenshire, Elizabeth Adamson, daughter of Gilbert Adamson in Kindrought, was born on 5 July 1691, and baptised by George Keith. Godfathers were George Peirie in Kindrought and James Gleny the younger (DUA.KLOC.54).

Stirling Archives has the records of Holy Trinity, Stirling, 1804-2004, and those of St. Saviour's in Bridge of Allan, 1855-1999. Shetland Archives has the records of St. Magnus Episcopal Church in Lerwick (ZA.D54).

## ROMAN CATHOLIC CHURCH

The Reformation in Scotland dates from 1560, when Scotland became officially a Protestant country and Roman Catholicism was banished. However, a Catholic presence remained in existence, albeit underground. The Stuart kings unsuccessfully attempted to convert the Scots from Calvinism to Episcopalianism, which led to the Covenanter Risings and eventually the Stuarts losing their thrones. The Jacobite Rebellions of 1689, 1709, 1715, and 1745 were attempts to restore the Stuarts to their thrones and were supported by Episcopalians and Roman Catholics in Scotland. This led to both denominations being subjected to penal laws that essentially made their churches illegal, with exception, hence the virtual absence of comprehensive records for most of the eighteenth century.

Roman Catholic enclaves could be found in certain Highland glens, such as at Braemar and Glenlivet; in the West Highlands; some of the Hebridean islands, such as Barra; and down in the South West of Scotland; however, location changed mainly with the influx from Ireland during the nineteenth century.

***Publications.*** Possibly the best source book is *Scottish Catholic Family History* (Andrew R. Nicoll, Edinburgh, 2011). The records identified in the book are mostly from mid-nineteenth century; exceptions include St. Mary's Cathedral, Edinburgh, 1777; St. Peter's, Buckie, 1786; Braemar, 1608- ; Bellie, Banffshire, 1785- ; Blairs/Scalan, 1789- ; Ballater, 1769- ; Aberdeen, 1774- ; Huntly, 1742; Glasgow, 1792 - ; Fort William, 1794- ; Eskdale, 1793 - ; Dalbeattie, 1745- ; and Crieff, 1799- .

Publications listing Scottish Catholics include Frances McDonnell's *Scottish Catholics and their Children 1701-1705* (St. Andrews, 1995), which is based on lists in the NRS; *The Catholic Church in Modern Scotland, from 1560 to 1937* (Peter Anson, 1937); and *Modern Scottish Catholicism* (David McRoberts, 1979).

An example of the type of entry to be found in David Dobson's *Scottish Catholics at Home and Abroad, 1680-1780* (Baltimore, 2010) follows:

> John McIntyre, born 1783 in South Uist, died 18
> November 1857 on Cape Breton Island, his wife
> Catherine, born 1785 on South Uist, died 13 July 1857
> on Cape Breton Island (St. Andrew's R.C. Cemetery,
> Boisdale, Cape Breton, Nova Scotia).

***Records in Archives.*** The Scottish Catholic Archives are partially located at Columba House, 16 Drummond Place, Edinburgh (**www.scottish catholicarchives.org.uk**). It holds substantial records of Catholicism in

Scotland, including the papers of several Catholic families. The National Records of Scotland has some lists of Catholics, such as "A list of unruly Papists in Marr (Aberdeenshire) 29 April 1703" (NRS.CH1.2.5.3). As mentioned in the previous chapter, many Catholic records have been digitally imaged and are now viewable on the ScotlandsPeople website (**www.scotlandspeople.gov.uk**).

## SOCIETY OF FRIENDS

Quakerism came to Scotland with the Cromwellian Army of Occupation of the 1650s. The Army was purged of Friends in 1657, and some of these men became early missionaries in Scotland. By the late seventeenth century, meeting houses had been established in four districts in Scotland. In North East Scotland, Friends were located in Aberdeen and in the nearby hamlets of Kinmuck and Ury. In South East Scotland, Friends were found in and around Edinburgh as well as in Kelso, while Hamilton, near Glasgow, was the site in West Scotland. Apart from these locations, individual Quakers and their families could be found in Montrose and Burntisland.

These early Quakers were persecuted by both the Presbyterians and the Episcopalians, which led to an exodus of most of them to East New Jersey in the 1680s. Despite this, the Society of Friends maintained a presence in Scotland.

*Publications.* *The Story of Quakerism in Scotland, 1650-1850* (G. Burnet, London, 1952), and David Dobson's *Scottish Quakers and Early America, 1650-1700* (Baltimore, 1998).

*Records in Archives.* Most of the records of the Society of Friends were transcribed by A. Strath-Maxwell, and his typescript lists, entitled "Scottish Quaker Records from the 17th Century to the 19th Century," are available for consultation in the National Records of Scotland in Edinburgh. Glasgow City Archives has births, marriages, and deaths, as well as proposals of marriages, in the records of the local Society of Friends. It also has a copy of a register containing an alphabetical list of members of the Edinburgh meeting, 1788-1965, which gives name, designation, where recommended from, and where removed to (GCA.TD204).

## SMALLER DENOMINATIONS

There are several smaller denominations in Scotland, such as the Brethren, that are difficult to track. There were various types of Brethren, including the "Closed," "Open," or "Exclusive" Brethren. They tended to be found in fishing villages along the northeastern coast. Another small denomination is the Churches of Christ—their earliest congregation was established in Auchtermuchty in 1807.

Thomas Campbell and his son Alexander were influential in the development of dissenting churches that merged into the Churches of Christ, which had congregations in Glasgow, Dundee, Perth, Banff, Turriff, Edinburgh, Cupar, Dunfermline, Montrose, and Dumfries by 1840. In 1981 most of the surviving churches joined the United Reform Church. The Moravians had a brief presence in Scotland with a church in Ayr around 1765, another in nearby Irvine in 1771, and one in Glasgow in the mid-nineteenth century.

*Publications.* "Researching the Brethren Movement in Scotland. Problems and Possibilities" (in *Scottish Archives*, volume 15, pages 42-56); "The Moravian Brethren in Scotland" (in *Register of the Scottish Church History Society*, volume 5/1, pages 50-72). A rare record of secular marriages is *Marriages at Gretna Hall from 1829 to 1855* (E. W. J. McConnel, Edinburgh, 1949), which deals with runaway marriages, often elopements, from England in the early nineteenth century.

## FREEMASONRY

*Publications.* *The Scottish Origins of Freemasonry* (David Stevenson, Edinburgh, 1987); *Scottish Masonic Records, from 1736 to 1950* (George S. Draffen, Edinburgh, 1950); *History of the Lodge of Edinburgh, number 1* (D. Murray Lyon, Edinburgh, 1900); *A History of the Mason Lodge of Holyrood House, no.44* (R. S. Lindsay, Edinburgh, 1935), which has a list of members 1734-1934; *Lodge Kirkwall Kilwinning from 1736* (J. Flett, Lerwick, 1976); and *History of the Ancient Masonic Lodge of Scoon and Perth, no.3* (D. C. Smith, Perth,1898).

## JUDAISM

There has been a Jewish presence, albeit small-scale, in Scotland for over 200 years. The majority were Ashkenazi Jews from Russia, Poland, and the Baltic states in the late nineteenth century, and subsequently others from Germany and other parts of Europe in the 1930s and 1940s. Many arrived via east coast ports such as Aberdeen, Dundee, and Leith (the port of Edinburgh, which had long established trading links with the Baltic). The main center of settlement seems to have been Glasgow. Currently, there are around 4,500 Jews in Scotland. The Scottish Jewish Heritage Centre, based at the Garnethill Synagogue, 129 Hill Street, Glasgow, G3 6UB (**www.sjac.org.uk**), is the best source in Scotland for Jewish family history.

***Publications***. K. E. Collins' *The Second City Jewry. The Jews of Glasgow in the Age of Expansion, 1790-1919* (Glasgow, 1990); *The Jewish Presence in Early British Records, 1650-1850* (David Dobson, Baltimore, 2014); *A History of the Origins of the First Jewish Community in Scotland* (Abel Phillips, Edinburgh, 1979).

# Chapter 4

# SECONDARY SOURCES

## Monumental Inscription Lists

Gravestones and monumental inscriptions contain a wealth of information for the family historian. This primary source of data is of particular importance to Scottish genealogists because the Old Parish Registers of the Church of Scotland concentrate on baptism and marriage and contain little on burial. The only clue to burials in the Kirk's records lies in the parish Kirk Session registers, where income from the rentals of the parish mortcloths may be recorded.

*Publications.* Virtually every graveyard and church in Scotland has had their monumental inscriptions transcribed and published. Some were compiled by individuals and others by local family history societies. Some of the earlier books were restricted to pre-1855 inscriptions, on the basis that statutory registration of births, marriages, and deaths began in Scotland that year; examples of such publications are A. Mitchell's *Speyside pre-1855 Monumental Inscriptions* (Edinburgh, 1974) and *Inverness West District, pre-1855 Monumental Inscriptions* (A. G. & M. Beattie, Edinburgh, 1993). Most of the more recent publications, however, include inscriptions dating into the mid-twentieth century, notably those published by the Aberdeen and North East Scotland Family History Society and the Scottish Genealogy Society.

Early Dundee gravestones *(courtesy of the Scottish Genealogy Society)*

Monumental inscriptions are particularly useful in that they sometimes record the death of a family member abroad, including those abroad on military service. The following are examples:

> John Balfour Kirk, born 3 April 1863, son of John
> Balfour Kirk, MD (1826-1882) and his wife Jessie Ingram
> Arthur (1829-1897), who died on 11 August 1888 and
> was buried in Fairview Cemetery, Stillwater, USA (a
> Boghead gravestone in Bathgate), or Robert Kerr, born
> 1829, son of Robert Kerr and his wife Agnes Haldane,
> a Congregationalist minister in Tonah, Kansas, died
> in Wakefield, Kansas, on 29 June 1890 (a Kilmarnock
> gravestone).

and

> Catherine McLean, born 1809, daughter of Kenneth
> McLean and his wife Jean McVicar, died in St Johns,
> Newfoundland, on 22 March 1866 (Greenock gravestone,
> Renfrewshire).

These, and similar entries, can be found in *Scottish American Gravestones, 1700-1900* (David Dobson, Baltimore, 1998, 2016), which concentrates, as the title states, on inscriptions that contain a transatlantic element. Sometimes several generations can be found in close proximity; for example, in Gullane Kirkyard in East Lothian are the following inscriptions:

> John William Yule, born 1800, son of James Yule, born
> 1759, died at Luffness Mill on 3 July 1837 and his wife
> Alison Dudgeon, died on the Ganges on 14 November
> 1848 and was buried at Bhaugulpore, also that of Colonel
> Robert Abercromby Yule, third son of Major William
> Yule, was killed at Delhi at the head of his regiment,
> the 9th Lancers, on 19 June 1857 during the Sepoy
> Revolt, his wife Margaret, born 24 September 1816,
> died in Ealing on 13 August 1903; and William Yule,
> born 22 September 1764, a Major in the Service of the
> Honourable East India Company, died on 4 October
> 1839, husband of Elizabeth Patterson, born 22 April
> 1785, died 24 February 1829.

Gravestone with Biblical significance *(Abraham gravestone – Lundie Graveyard, Angus)*

Gravestone with merchant mark *(Greyfriars Graveyard, Edinburgh)*

The early publications often only listed gravestones dating before 1855, as the post-1855 statutory sources provided the basic information, but nowadays almost everything is noted, especially the overseas data. The books of monumental inscriptions have been researched by members of the various family history societies in Scotland and are available from them. The urgency of the work results from the fact that many stones are crumbling away, while others have been subject to vandalism or to destruction by the local government clearing graveyards prior to "development," as happened to the Constitution Street, Dundee, graveyard. The existence of such sourcebooks is of great benefit to researchers because many of the graveyards lie in remote and difficult-to-access locations. Monumental inscription books can be found in most reference libraries in Scotland or from the various Scottish family history societies.

Many seventeenth- and eighteenth-century gravestones found in Scottish graveyards have a feature called "trade symbols." For example, the symbol of the hammermen (i.e., the metal trades) is the royal crown above a hammer, while a "4" indicates the grave of a merchant. These are described and explained in Betty Willsher's illustrated publication *Understanding Scottish Graveyards,* which was published in Edinburgh in 1995; also see her *Stones, 18th Century Scottish Gravestones* (Edinburgh, 1978). Also worthwhile is Hamish Brown's *A Scottish Graveyard Miscellany. Exploring the Folk Art of Scotland's Gravestones* (Edinburgh, 2008).

**Other Sources.** The only other major sources of gravestone information lie in the obituary columns of the press or in the various Registers of Testaments.

# STATISTICAL ACCOUNTS OF SCOTLAND

In 1790 Sir John Sinclair, a noted agricultural improver, persuaded the ministers of all parishes in Scotland to prepare reports on their parish with information on a broad range of topics, including population, the local economy, industries, churches, and landowners during the 1790s. *The Statistical Account of Scotland, 1791-1799* is available in published form (Sir John Sinclair, Wakefield, EP Publishing, 1973-83) as well as in a digitized version accessible at the National Library of Scotland. It is said to be the best European contemporary record of life during the agricultural and industrial revolutions. It provides an insight into the economy and society of every parish in the land.

The National Library of Scotland website has a section called "The Scottish Enlightenment" (**https://digital.nls.uk/learning/scottish-enlightenment/statistical-account/**), which contains part of the reports for the parishes of Monymusk, Wick, Culross, East Kilbride, and Smailholm, providing good examples of what to expect from the Statistical Account. It is a must if you want insight into the society that your ancestor experienced at the end of the eighteenth century.

In 1845 an updated *New Statistical Account of Scotland* was compiled and published based on reports compiled between 1834 and 1845. An earlier source covering similar ground was produced by the Reverend Alexander Webster in 1755. In 1952 the Scottish History Society published *Scottish Population Statistics* based on Webster's work (**www.nrscotland.gov.uk/files/research/census-records/websters-census-of-1755-scottish-population-statistics.pdf**).

## HERITORS' RECORDS

Since the Reformation of 1560, the landowners in each parish were responsible for the maintenance of the parish church and the minister's stipend, a manse and glebe, a churchyard and school, and the poor. The landowners were the heritors, and they imposed a tax on lands within the parish to finance all of this. Within the burghs, the heritors were the magistrates. The Heritors' Records survive for most parishes for the nineteenth century, many for the eighteenth century, and a few for the seventeenth century.

***Records in Archives.*** Heritors' Records can be found in the National Records of Scotland. One of the earliest to survive is that of the parish of Fenwick, which dates from 1623 (NRS.HR641). Others include the Records of the Heritors' of Abercorn from 1702 to 1930 (NRS.HR.16); the Records of the Heritors' of Minnigaff from 1667 to 1925 (NRS.

HR282); and the Records of the Heritors' of Linlithgow from 1678 to 1930 (NRS.HR78). An example of this type of record:

> On 9 October 1682 there was a commission by the heritors of the parish of Errol to Andrew Drummond of Megginch, Peter Hay of Leys, John Blair of Balmyle, and George Oliphant of Clashbervie to inspect the fabric of the church, school, and schoolhouse and raise money for their repair (NRS.B59.28.44).

The power and influence of the heritors contributed to certain Presbyterian churches breaking from the Church of Scotland.

# TAX RECORDS

## The Hearth Tax

The Hearth Tax was authorized by Parliament in 1690 on every hearth in the land. The objective was to raise money to pay for loans received from the burghs and the army (Acts of the Parliaments of Scotland.ix.236). Between 1694 and 1699 the Hearth Tax was levied on the head of every household, and charges were for each hearth in the home. No one was exempt, apart from those under 16 years old or the very poor. These records provide vital data on residents throughout Scotland in the closing years of the seventeenth century. The records, on a county basis, are in the National Records of Scotland. The Hearth Tax rolls from Exchequer records (NRS reference E69) are available online on the ScotlandsPlaces website (**https://scotlandsplaces.gov.uk/**).

***Publications.*** A few of these tax records have been published, for example, *The West Lothian Hearth Tax, 1691* (D. Adamson, Edinburgh, 1981); *The Hearth Tax for Ayrshire, 1691* (R. Urquhart and R. Close, Ayr, 1998); *The Perthshire Hearth Tax of 1691-1692* (Karl Ransome, Edinburgh, 2001); "The Hearth Tax of Dumfriesshire, 1691" (Duncan Adamson in *Transactions of the Dumfries and Galloway Natural History and Antiquarian Society*, 3rd series, volume 47); and *Sutherland Hearth Tax, 1691* (A. S. Cowper, Edinburgh, 1985). Those for Angus alias Forfarshire of 1691 were published in five parts by David Dobson (St. Andrews, 2006-2007).

*Records in Archives.* The NRS has the Hearth Tax records for Dunbartonshire (NRS.E69.7.1); Dumfriesshire (NRS.E69.8.1); East Lothian (NRS.E69.9.1); Edinburgh (NRS.E69.69.16/1-3); Elgin (NRS.E69.17); Fife (NRS.E69.10.1/2); Forestshire (NRS.E69.18); Angus (NRS. E69.11.1); Galloway (NRS.E69.25); Haddington (NRS.E69.9); Inverness-shire (NRS.E69.12.1); Kincardineshire (NRS.E69.13.1); Kirkcudbright (NRS.E69.14.1); Lanarkshire (NRS.E69.15.1/2); Moray & Nairn (NRS.E69.17.1); Peebles-shire and Selkirkshire (NRS.E69.18.1); Perthshire (NRS.E69.19.1-2); East Renfrewshire (NRS.E69.20.1); Roxburghshire (NRS.E69.21.1); Stirlingshire (NRS.E69.22.1); Sutherland (NRS. E69.23.1); West Lothian (NRS.E69.24.1/2); Argyll and Bute (NRS. GD26.7.38); Dunbartonshire (NRS.GD26.7.380); Dumfriesshire (NRS. GD26.7.375); Ross-shire (NRS.RH2.8.21; NRS.GD305.271/272/280); and Shetland (NRS.RH1.2.821).

## The Poll Tax

The Poll Tax was imposed by Parliament in 1693. The funds raised were to reduce the national debt, including army arrears. A second Poll Tax was introduced in 1695 to raise money for the Royal Navy. The Poll Tax records are mostly in the National Records of Scotland. Poll Tax records from the 1690s are now available online on the ScotlandsPlaces website (**https://scotlandsplaces.gov.uk/**).

*Publications.* List of Pollable Persons within the Shire of Aberdeen, 1696, two volumes (Spalding Club, Aberdeen, 1844); *Transactions of the Banffshire Field Club*, 1903, pp. 3-18, for those deficient in 1695; *Renfrewshire in the 1690s, Hearth and Poll Taxes* (J. Malden, Paisley, 2000); *The Orkney Poll Taxes of the 1690s* ( J. M. Irvine, Ashtead, 2003); *Edinburgh Poll Tax Returns for 1694* (Margaret Wood, Edinburgh, 1951); *Burgh of Paisley, Poll Tax Roll, 1695* (F. McDonnell, St. Andrews, 1995); "Paisley Poll Tax Roll, 1695," in *A History of Paisley* (W. M. Metcalfe, Paisley, 1909).

*Records in Archives.* Poll Tax lists include those from Ayrshire, 1698 (NRS.E70.1.1/2); Berwickshire, 1698 (NRS.E70.2.1/2); East Lothian, partial (NRS.E70.3.1); Edinburgh, Canongate, and Leith, 1691, 1694, 1695, 1698 (NRS.E70.4.1-12); Fife, 1698, 1699 (NRS.E70.5.1-9);

Inverness-shire (NRS.E70.6.1); Lanarkshire, 1698 (NRS.E70.7.1-5); Midlothian, 1694, 1695 (NRS.E70.8.1-19); Nairnshire, 1699 (NRS. E70.9.1); Orkney, 1699 (NRS.E70.10.1); Perthshire, 1699 (NRS. E70.11.1); Renfrewshire, 1694, 1695, 1696 (NRS.E.70.12.1-9); West Lothian, 1694, 1695, 1699 (NRS.E70.13.1-8); Wigtownshire, 1699 (NRS.E70.14.1). Also, Aberdeenshire (NRS.GD52.6/7/8); Argyll, 1698, 1699 (NRS.SC54.20.1); Berwickshire, 1695 (NRS.305.1.164/273, NRS.GD86.770A, NRS.GD158.679); Fife (NRS.RH2.1.68); Upper Ward of Lanarkshire, 1695 (National Register of Archives, Scotland); Orkney, 1690, 1693, 1694, 1695, 1696 (NRS.RH9.15.175.1/2); Peebles-shire, 1690s (NRS.SC42.46.1); Perthshire, 1695, 1696 (NRS. GD316.10; NRS.GD56.128; Perth and Kinross Archives.ms79.259); Renfrewshire, 1695 (NRS.T335/T345/T346); Ross-shire, 1690s (NRS. GD305.1.164.273); Selkirkshire, 1695 (NRS.GD178, box 2/bundle 1).

Edinburgh City Archives has the local Poll Tax returns from 1694 to 1699 (ECA.SL225).

## Valuation Rolls

In 1854 the Lands Valuation (Scotland) Act was passed, which authorized local authorities to annually compile lists of every heritable property, giving its location, description, name of owner, tenant or occupier, and value. The object was to establish a uniform basis for local government taxation. Valuation Rolls provide information for years that fall between census years and for years after 1911, the last year for which census records are currently available to family historians. The website **www.scotlandspeople.gov.uk** is the best single source for Valuation Rolls between 1855 and 1940.

***Records in Archives and Libraries.*** These records are partly in the NRS and partly in local archives. The NRS has the county and burgh Valuation Rolls covering the period 1855 to 1975 (NRS.VR.1-148). The Valuation Rolls for Aberdeen City exist from 1855, for Aberdeenshire from 1859, for Kincardine from 1862, for Banff from 1877, and for Moray from 1902—all these are in the Aberdeen City Archives at Old Aberdeen House. Shetland Archives has the local Valuation Rolls and

Voters Rolls from 1832 (ZA.CO.8). Dundee Reference Library has those for Angus and Dundee; those for Edinburgh can be consulted in the Edinburgh Central Library, while those for Glasgow are in the Mitchell Library. The Mitchell Library has a computerized Valuation Roll Index for the years 1832, 1861, 1881, and 1911, which also lists the occupation of the householder.

## Miscellaneous Taxes

During the late eighteenth century the British Government imposed a range of taxes, mainly to finance the British army and navy during the American and French wars. These taxes tended to be levied on the more affluent in society.

*Records in Archives.* The NRS has tax records for Midlothian (NRS. E327 and E920), including land tax collection books, 1735-1803; income tax assessments, 1799-1801; property tax assessments, 1803-12; small house duty collections books, 1803-12; militia and reserve army, deficiency assessments, 1805; and cash books and ledgers for payments to militia wives and families, 1803-15.

Land Tax Rolls, listing the owners of landed estates and rental value of their lands, were compiled in each county to facilitate the collection of the land tax. Rolls, 1645-1831, submitted to the Scottish Exchequer (NRS reference E106) are available online on the ScotlandsPlaces website (**www.scotlandsplaces.gov.uk**). Other Land Tax Rolls can be found among Commissioners of Supply records in local archives.

The Window Tax was charged on houses with more than seven windows. There are Window Tax records for the burghs in 1748, 1753 to 1798 (NRS.E326.1.126-218), and for the counties from 1748 to 1798, with exceptions (NRS.E326.1.1-124). The Male Servants Tax provides the names of servants, 1777-1798 (NRS.E326.5); the Inhabited House Tax provides the names of householders, 1778-1798 (NRS.E326.3); the Cart Tax lists cart-owners, 1785-1792 (NRS.326.7); the Carriage Tax lists carriage owners, 1785-1798 (NRS.E326.8); the Horse Tax identifies those who owned carriage and saddle-horses, 1785-1798 (NRS.E326.9); the Female Servants Tax identifies the names of the masters and their female servants (NRS.E326.6); the Farm Horse Tax gives numbers of horses and the owners' names (NRS.E326.10). These records and others are available in the NRS and are organized by county. NRS has begun uploading some of these householders' taxes rolls to the ScotlandsPlaces website (**www.scotlandsplaces.gov.uk**). For more detailed information about the NRS tax records, visit **https://www.nrscotland.gov.uk/research/ guides/taxation-records**.

Female servants' tax list *(courtesy of National Records of Scotland)*

## SASINES AND LAND REGISTERS

The Scottish Registers of Sasines are among the oldest continuing records of land transactions in Europe. A sasine is a document recording that a piece of land or a building had changed hands, usually by a sale or an inheritance. The system in Scotland was formalized in 1617 with the foundation of the Register of Sasines. Before then, property records were kept by notaries. Registers of Sasines exist for the Royal Burghs and for rural areas or sheriffdoms from 1617 until 1870, when a General Register of Sasines on a county basis was introduced. Since 1979 the Registers of Sasines have been replaced by a Land Register on a county basis.

***Publications and Records in Archives.*** There are published Sasine Abridgements from 1781 available in printed form, indexed alphabetically by surnames and organized on a county basis. Indexes to the Particular Register of Sasines for every county or sheriffdom are also available, generally dating from the early seventeenth century to 1780. These publications can be accessed in the NRS (see **www.nrscotland. gov.uk/research/guides/sasines** for a list of records held by the NRS) and in major archives.

Many of the burgh Registers of Sasines can also be accessed in the NRS, though some are in local archives, for example *Index to Secretary's Register of Sasines for Sheriffdoms of Edinburgh, Haddington, Linlithgow, and Bathgate, 1599-1609* (Edinburgh, 1959); and *Index to Particular Register of Sasines for Sheriffdom of Forfar*, Vol. 1, 1620-1700 (Edinburgh, 1965), and Vol. 2, 1701-1780 (Edinburgh, 1989). These cover the rural areas, while the burghs had their own internal registers.

In 2000 the system of feudal land tenure was finally abolished in Scotland, taking effect in 2004. Now a nationwide Land Register records all property transactions. Under the feudal system all land was owned by the king, who would grant land to selected subjects to hold and develop in exchange for loyalty and military service, when required. If the individual became a rebel, then the land would be reclaimed by the king, who would then allocate it to a more loyal person. On the death of a person holding land, the land did not automatically go to the heir but was, in theory, returned to the king, who could allocate it to the heir of the deceased or grant it to some other individual. Such land grants were recorded in the Register of the Great Seal of Scotland, which was published in eleven volumes covering the period 1306 to 1668. A digitized version can be viewed at **https://catalog.hathitrust.org/Record/010478724.** All volumes are in Latin except the last two from 1651 to 1668, which are in English; an excerpt follows:

> Charter granting to David Moir of Craggarmill, clerk to
> the sheriffdom of Stirling, his heirs and assignees—half of

> the lands and barony of Leckie, commonly called Wester
> Leckie, contiguous to the lands and barony of Boquhan,
> extending to a £10 land of old extent, with mill, mill-
> lands, multures, fortalice, houses and buildings, tenants,
> services, etc., in the sheriffdom of Stirling; formerly
> belonging to John Leckie of that Ilk, held by service of
> ward and relief, and now fallen into the Crown's hand by
> recognition:- rendering therefor yearly the service of ward
> and relief; with precept of sasine:- witnesses' names not
> engrossed. Edinburgh, 12 July 1668 (RMS.XI.1194).

The Register of the Great Seal volumes are well indexed by names and places. Copies, especially the 1984 reprint by Clark Constable in Edinburgh, London, and Melbourne, are available in major libraries. There is also a Register of Tailzie in the NRS. Sometimes a family, in order to keep the property within the family, had it "entailed," which meant that only a male member of the family could inherit it. If the sole heir was a married woman, her husband had to adopt the family surname to keep the property. This was codified by the Entail Act of 1685.

## SERVICES OF HEIRS, ALIAS "RETOURS"

When a landowner died, the local sheriff would hold an inquest to establish the credentials of any person claiming to be the true and rightful heir to lands that were in the possession of the deceased at the time of his or her death. The documentary evidence associated with the inquest is known as the Services of Heirs and is a valuable genealogical source. Indexes to the Services of Heirs, alias "Retours," were published for the period 1530 to 1700 under the title *Inquisition ad Capellam Regis Retornatarum Abbreviato* (Edinburgh, Great Britain Record Commission, 1811-1816). These are in Latin, whereas the indexes from 1701 until the present day are in English. Such indexes can be found in major libraries, such as the National Library of Scotland, the National Records of Scotland, or in the older universities of Scotland.

*Publications*. The only publication dealing with a particular county is *The Services of Heirs, Roxburghshire, from 1636 to 1847* (John MacLeod, Edinburgh, 1934), which has listings such as:

> The General Service of Andrew Jerdan, gardener at
> Paston, to his father Andrew Jerdan, gardener at Bongate,
> second son of the deceased Andrew Jerdan the elder,
> gardener at Bongate, 24 July 1770.

Extracts from the Services of Heirs, which identify residents of the United States, Canada, and the West Indies, are listed in David Dobson's *Scottish American Heirs, 1684-1883* (Baltimore, 1990). Examples found in Dobson's book include:

> Frederick William Minniken Watt in Poughkeepsie,
> New York, who was served heir to his mother Elizabeth
> Henry, widow of George Watt in Turriff, Aberdeenshire,
> who died on 22 February 1891 .... Richard Wardrop in
> St Louise, Missouri, who was served heir to his mother
> Jessie Whyte Glenor Wardrop in London, who died on 15
> March 1882.

Researchers with origins in Fife will find the publications of Andrew J. Campbell extremely useful. Among them are two books based on local newspapers, namely *Fife Deaths, 1822-1854* and *Fife Deaths Abroad, 1855-1900*, which can be found in most libraries in Fife. A digital download of *Fife Deaths Abroad, 1855-1900* is available at **https://fifefhs.org/product/fife-deaths-abroad-1855-1900-digital-download/**.

## BARONY COURT BOOKS

From about 1200 onward the Scottish kings established administrative units known as baronies. These baronies were supervised by lords known as barons, whose functions included ensuring that the king's laws operated within the barony, collecting taxes, maintaining a Barony Court where local justice was administered, and also providing the king with a number of knights and men when required. By the late seventeenth century there were around one thousand baronies in Scotland. The records of these baronial courts, where they have survived, provide a unique insight into the social and economic life of the barony.

A barony was granted, generally, for a lifetime but could be withdrawn by the king if the baron was a rebel. On the death of a baron the land theoretically returned to the Crown but was then issued to his heir. Though baronies still exist, the power of the barons was broken in 1747 with the Heritable Jurisdiction Act, which was designed to stop barons legally leading their tenants into a rebellion, as had happened with the Jacobites in 1745.

***Publications.*** One of the few Barony Court books to be published is *The Records of the Baron Court of Stitchill, 1655-1807* (G. Gunn, Edinburgh, 1905). A sample entry is as follows:

> At the Head Barron Court held at Stitchill Kirk on
> 23 August 1662 before the baron Robert Pringle of
> Stitchill—William Taylor in Queenscairn is required to
> pay to the kirk treasurer to be employed ad pios usos
> five merks Scots for Nicola Wood being her penalty for
> her former scolding and the like misbehaviour, who
> was arrested by him as her debtor at the instance of the
> kirk session. Nicola has undertaken to live peaceably
> in all time coming under the pain of twenty pounds
> and banishment from the barony. (modern transcript);
> later, at Stitchill, on 18 May 1725, George Hamilton,
> David Hogarth, John Miller, James Aitchison, Simon
> Marjorybanks, Joan Innes, and Alexander Hyslop,
> residents in Stitchill, were fined for not having paid their
> share of Andrew Whale, the schoolmaster's salary, and
> were penalised ten shillings Scots.

Another published book is *The Court Book of the Barony of Urie, 1604-1747* (R. G. Barron, Edinburgh, 1892), which records the following:

> At the Baron Court of Urie, pertaining to Robert Barclay
> the younger, held in the manor place thereof on 30
> February 1731, by Alexander Brown in the Mains of Urie,
> bailie James Milne NP a clerk, John Soutar the fiscal,
> William Cairn the dempster, and William Thomson
> court officer, in the presence of the laird. An action
> against John Smith, servant to the laird of Urie accused of
> hurting, wounding and blood drawing of John and James
> Davidson, brothers in Muchalls, and Alexander Davidson
> and William Henderson, all in Muchalls, at Cransacre in
> February 1730.

Occasionally, a printed source contains extracts from a Barony Court book; see, for example, William Fraser's *Cartulary of the Colquhouns of Luss* (Edinburgh, 1873), which has part of the court book of the Barony of Luss dating between 1663 and 1792. The Forbes Barony Court book, dating between 1659 and 1678, was published in Volume XIX of the Scottish History Society publications in 1919.

***Records in Archives.*** Most Barony Court books are unpublished. Some are found in local or national archives. The Guthries were barons of Guthrie in Angus from the medieval period. The family was generally Royalist and supporters of the House of Stuart. As barons of Guthrie they were required to support the king when required, and their tenants had to follow the baron into battle. During the Covenanter Risings the Guthries checked on the loyalties of their tenants; for example, according to the Barony Court book of Guthrie, "in 1686, Charles Air in Heughheid undertook not to become a 'fanatick'" (that is a Covenanter) (NRS. GD188.31.11).

Many Barony Court records and other documents dealing with the barony remain in the archives of landowners. However, there are a number available for consultation in the NRS. These include the baronies of Courthill from 1666 to 1719 (NRS.GD1.300.1); Abercairney from 1689 to 1762 (NRS.GD24.1.602); Drummond from 1712 to 1717 (NRS. GD24.1.781); Lude from 1621 to 1908 (NRS.GD50.169); Broxmouth and Pinkerton from 1620 to 1764 (NRS.GD100.289); Abernethy, Cromdale, and Urquhart from 1617 to 1683 (NRS.GD248.76.2); Monymusk from 1710 to 1771 (NRS.GD345-786); Edinbellie, from 1623 to 1793 (NRS.GD1.223); Skene from 1613 to 1655 (NRS.GD1.299); Logie Wishart from 1681 to 1738 (NRS.GD1.339); Guthrie from 1666 to 1719 (NRS.GD1.188); Leckie and Culbeg from 1687 to 1724 (NRS. GD1.132); various processes from the Barony Courts in Caithness, including the Earl of Breadalbane's Baron Court held in Thurso in 1709 (NRS.SC14.69.3); inventories from the Dunkeld Courts from 1682 to 1809 (NRS.SC49.74.1); and the Baron Baillie Courts of Argyll in 1747 (NRS.SC54.27).

Throughout Scotland, Barony Court books can also be found in local archives. For example, the National Library of Scotland has the Barony Court book of Calder from 1584 to 1601 (NLS.ms3724-5); Aberdeen University Library has the Barony Court book of Philorth from 1653 to 1676 (AUL.ms2867); Dumfries and Galloway Archives has the Barony Court book of Logan and Clanyard from 1739 to 1806 (DGA. GGD.108); Angus Archives has the Barony Court book of Balmadies from 1600 to 1629 (AA.ms322.2); and Glasgow City Archives has the Barony Court book of Gorbals, from 1700 to 1716 (GCA-H.GOR).

Possibly the earliest Barony Court book to exist is that of Fowlis in Gowrie (HMC.mss.Com. Rep.III, App.410); another is that of the barony of Cambusnethan in Lanarkshire, referred to in Andrew Stuart's *Genealogical History of the Stewarts*, page 96. Drummond Castle Archives are said to contain the Barony Court books of Auchterarder, Drummond in Lennox, and Kincardine in Menteith from the sixteenth century.

## WILLS AND TESTAMENTS

In Scotland inheritance is controlled by a testament, a term used to describe all the documents relating to the estate of a deceased person, while a will is a particular document in a testament. Assets are of two types: heritable, which consist of land and buildings; and movable, which refers to anything that can be physically transported, often referred to as "goods, gear, sums of money, and debts." Before 1868 wills could transfer only moveable property, not heritable property. A 1964 act canceled these restrictions.

A *testament testamentar* is when the deceased left a will (i.e., testate), and when no will was left (intestate), a *testament dative* is drawn up by the court, formerly by the Commissary Court (Commissariat), now by the Sheriff Court. Prior to the Reformation, this function was fulfilled by the local diocese of the Roman Catholic Church, but in 1564 Commissary Courts were established for that purpose. There were thirteen, later twenty-two, Commissary Courts, which were created based on the former dioceses, with one in Edinburgh that had jurisdiction throughout Scotland and was also available to Scots dying abroad. Note that Scots living abroad sometimes registered their wills there, and any in England or in an English colony could use the Prerogative Court of Canterbury. You may also find wills and testaments recorded in Registers of Deeds. The surviving wills, before 1800, have been indexed and published by the Scottish Record Society, organized by Commissary and in alphabetical order. Some of these books are still available from the Society. Most reference libraries in Scotland have copies, and the contents of the books can be seen in digitized form on the website of the Scottish Record Society (**www.scottish recordsociety.org.uk/**). Testaments 1514-1925 have been digitally imaged and can be viewed in the ScotlandsPeople Centre and in the National Records of Scotland Historical Search Room. Copies of these images are available for purchase on the ScotlandsPeople website (**www. scotlandspeople.gov.uk**), which also contains a full index to these testaments.

Below is a list of testaments from the various Commissary Courts, with sample extracts.

*Aberdeen Commissariat Testaments, Index, 1715-1800* (Francis J. Grant, Edinburgh, 1899):

> Jean Glass, widow of Duncan Cumming a merchant in
> Aberdeen, testament confirmed on 5 February 1729;
> also of Jane Patterson, late in Peterhead, widow of Joseph
> Johnston, sometime quartermaster of the 10th Regiment
> of Foot, testament confirmed on 11 October 1779).

*Argyle Commissariat Testaments, Index, 1674-1800* (Francis J. Grant, Edinburgh, 1902):

> Gilbert McArthur, overseer at the slate quarry at Esdale,
> testament confirmed on 12 March 1762; Margaret
> Lamont, eldest daughter of the deceased Dugald Lamont,
> and spouse of John Lamont of Kilfinan, testament
> confirmed on 18 May 1742.

*Brechin Commissariat Testaments, Index* (Francis J. Grant, Edinburgh, 1902):

Thomas Davidson, a merchant burgess of Dundee,
and his spouse Jean Kyd, testament confirmed on 23
March 1640; Alexander Cragtoun, alias Leslie, a tailor
in the North Ferry of Tay, parish of Dundee, and his
spouse Isobel Charterhouse, testament confirmed on 19
December 1651.

*Caithness Commissariat Testaments, Index, 1661-1664* (Francis J. Grant, Edinburgh, 1902):

Margaret Moir, daughter of Donald Moir, and spouse to
John McKurkullin in Tiubeg, testament confirmed in July
1663; Margaret Sinclair, spouse to John Nicoll a mariner
skipper in Thurso, testament confirmed on 17 February
1663.

*Dumfries Commissariat Testaments, Index, 1624-1800* (Francis J. Grant, Edinburgh, 1902):

Elizabeth Hunter, in Penpont, sometime spouse to
the deceased Patrick Boyle in Penpont, later spouse to
the deceased Richard Simonds in Penpont, testament
confirmed on 27 December 1793; William Wightman,
sometime a linen draper in Cheapside, London, thereafter
a resident of Dumfries, testament confirmed on 3 July
1771.

*Dunblane Commissariat Testaments, Index, 1539-1800* (Francis J. Grant, Edinburgh, 1902):

John McRobbie the younger, in Drummond, and his
spouse Mary Baillie, only daughter of the deceased Francis
Baillie a surgeon in Drummond, in the parish of Muthill,
testament confirmed on 6 September 1758; William
Monteith, late of the East Indies, testament confirmed on
15 December 1795.

*Dunkeld Commissariat Testaments, Index, 1682-1800* (Francis J. Grant, Edinburgh, 1902):

Alexander Ferguson, sometime in Ordchastle of
Duntaulich, eldest son of the deceased Alexander
Ferguson in Lavadge and his spouse Christian

McLauchlan, testament confirmed on 31 December 1772; John Dow, eldest son of the deceased Thomas Dow sometime in Balihomish and thereafter went abroad to Holland, testament confirmed on 20 November 1718.

*Edinburgh Commissariat Testaments, Indexes,* three volumes, 1514-1800 (Francis J. Grant, Edinburgh, 1898, 1902):

Charles Adair, a merchant in London, son of the deceased Charles Adair a merchant in Perth, testament confirmed on 11 May 1786, William Blair, a merchant burgess of Edinburgh, son of Cornet George Blair late of Hyndford's Dragoons, testament confirmed on 22 August 1723.

*Glasgow Commissariat Testaments, Index, 1547-1800* (Francis J. Grant, Edinburgh, 1901):

James Burns, ship carpenter in Port Glasgow, late carpenter aboard the ship *Port Glasgow,* William McClintock, commander, testament confirmed on 22 March 1754; Dr Alexander Wilson, Professor of Practical Astronomy at Glasgow University, testament confirmed on 2 December 1786 and on 28 August 1789.

*Hamilton and Campsie Commissariat Testaments, Index, 1564-1800* (Francis J. Grant, Edinburgh, 1897):

The testament of Ann Russell of Longridge, relict of Thomas Clarkson a merchant in Barbados, confirmed on 12 November 1773; and the testament of Geillis Slewman, spouse to Patrick Houstoun, a burgess of Dumbarton and then in the parish of Cardross, confirmed on 21 March 1618.

*Inverness Commissariat Testaments, Index, 1630-1800* (Francis J. Grant, Edinburgh, 1897):

The Testament of John McBean, late soldier in Lord John Murray's Regiment, son to William McBean, late tacksman of Kinapole, confirmed on 11 January 1749; also the Testament of Captain Alexander Mackenzie, of the Regiment commanded by General Marjorybanks, in the Service of the States General of the United Provinces, confirmed in July 1759.

*The Isles Commissariat Testaments, Index, 1661-1800* (Francis J. Grant, Edinburgh, 1902):

> Alexander Campbell of Kingsburgh, and James McDonald late tacksman of Knockow on Skye, testament confirmed on 20 May 1779; Neill McNeill, sometime a merchant on St. Kitts, later a resident of Ardtalley, Islay, testament confirmed on 4 February 1777.

*Kirkcudbright Commissariat Testaments, Index, 1663-1800* (Francis J. Grant, Edinburgh, 1903):

> Alexander McWhannell, Customs Officer at the port of Dumfries, testament confirmed in 1749; William Carsan, servant to the late William Maxwell the younger of Newlaw, testament confirmed in 1696.

*Lanark Commissariat Testaments, Index, 1595-1800* (Francis J. Grant, Edinburgh, 1903):

> Isobel Fleming, spouse to Gabriel Forrest portioner of Nether Langschaw, parish of Carluke; Adam Hislop in Sweitschaw, and his spouse Elizabeth Johnstoun, and their daughter Janet Hislop, in the parish of Crawford, testament confirmed on 3 October 1653; Thomas Carmichael, in Lanark, sometime adjutant in Lord Carmichael's Regiment of Dragoons, testament confirmed on 12 December 1709.

*Lauder Commissariat Testaments, Index, 1561-1800* (Francis J. Grant, Edinburgh, 1903):

> Andrew Brodie, schoolmaster of Abbey St. Bathuns, testament confirmed on 19 October 1736; Alison Dalgleish, relict of Gavin Melvill a merchant in Coldstream, testament confirmed on 26 February 1751; John Wemyss, of Lathokar, minister at Duns, testament confirmed in November 1636.

*Moray Commissariat Testaments, Index, 1684-1800* (Francis J. Grant, Edinburgh, 1904):

> John Leith, minister of the Episcopalian congregation in

Huntly and Jean Thomson his wife, testament confirmed on 27 August 1782; Alexander Dunbar of Westfield, the Sheriff of Moray, testament confirmed on 19 February 1704.

*Orkney and Shetland Commissariat Testaments, Index, 1611-1684* (Francis J. Grant, Edinburgh, 1904).

| | |
|---|---|
| 184 | *Commissariot of St. Andrews.* [1549-1800. |

Jolly, David, in Stonheave, and John and Robert Youngs, sons to the deceased John Youngs, in Logie, par. of Dunnottar — 22 Mar. 1723
„ David, Christian, William, and Katherine, lawful children of the deceased David Jollie, sometime in Balfeigh, thereafter in Stonehaven, par. of Dunnottar — 14 Aug. 1755
„ John, and Christian Garvie, at East Banff, in Arbuthnot — 13 Jan. 1800
Jonken, Isobel, spouse to James Bruce, in Mains of Ogill, par. of Tannadyce — 7 Jan. 1614
„ John, in Balbenie. *See* Carnegie, Barbara.
„ Robert, in Therniel. *See* Simpson, Margaret.
Jop, Alane — 17 Feb. 1595-6
„ James, in Kinloch. *See* Williamson, Margaret.
Jopsoun, Walter, maltman, burges of Dundee. *See* Lamb, Christian.
Jousie, Isabella, at Kinghorn Easter — . . Jan. 1550
Jowell, Christene, alias Dowgall, relict of Andrew Christie, in Caskyberrian, who dwelt in Auchmowtie, par. of Markinch — 9 July 1593
Joy, David, in Laws of Toments, par. of Logie — 13 Aug. 1662
„ John, in Three Laws. *See* Jap, Elspet.
„ Walter, in Three Laws of Dun, par. of Logie Montrose — 7 May 1618
Just, Isobel, spouse to Robert Millar, in Cruvie, par. of Logie — 13 June 1636
„ John, in Inchmichaell. *See* Anderson, Eupham.
„ John, in the Cottoun of Croovie. *See* Thrummond, Christian.
„ Rannald, in Sie-milns, par. of Forgund — 1 Dec. 1613
Justice, Agnes, spouse to John Carswell, par. of Cullessie — 17 July 1620
„ Alexander, in Newtoun of Cullessie, par. of Cullessie — 5 Aug. 1616
*See also* Henderson, Janet.
„ John, in Sherreftoun, par. of Scone — 23 July 1662
„ John, in Wester Elcho, par. of Rind. *See* Oliphant, Violet.
„ Ronald, in Sherefftoune. *See* Wilson, Barbara.
„ Thomas, in Dysart — 30 Dec. 1675
„ William, burges of Kirkcaldy — 12 May 1625
Kaas, Patrick, baxter, burges of Dysart — 13 Aug. 1641
Kaddie, Isobel, sometime spouse to Patrick Lessellis, husbandman in Newtown of Wemyss — 1 Aug. 1597
Kaid, Andrew, husbandman in Flisk-mylne. *See* Smart, Helen.
„ James, shepherd to the Earl of Crawfurd. *See* Richardson, Malie.
„ John, burges of Crail. *See* Bell, Elizabeth. — . . Jan. 1551
Kaivell, Bessie, alias Smith, sometime spouse to John Roger, tailor in Kirktoun of Erroll
Kandow, James, in Roughhaugh, par. of Lintrethan — 6 Apr. 1599
Kar, Gilbert, in Hoghillok, par. of Dunnottar — 18 Dec. 1793
„ Thomas, in Lochmiln — 1 June 1686
Karnye, Joneta, relict of Robert Pate, and the said Robert himself at St. Andrews — 29 Nov. 1588
Karrek, Helen, spouse to John Donaldsone, in Inchgall, par. of Ballingrie — . . Feb. 1550
Kay, Agnes, in Ferrietoune of Portincraig — 17 Apr. 1627
„ Agnes, widow at the Milne of ... — 22 Nov. 1606

List of testaments from St. Andrews *(courtesy of the Scottish Record Society)*

*Orkney Testaments and Inventories, 1573 -1615* (Robert S. Barclay, Edinburgh, 1977):

> The testament of Thomas Craik in Liddell on South
> Ronaldsay, who died in June 1602, by his widow Janet
> Beg, on behalf of his children Craiks, John, Malcolm,
> Thomas, Marion and Margaret, confirmed on 29 January
> 1614.

*Peebles Commissariat Testaments Index, 1681-1689* (Francis J. Grant, Edinburgh, 1902):

> Mark Pringle, eldest son of the late Robert Pringle of
> Clifton, testament confirmed on 21 January 1687;
> Thomas Spotswood in Shaiplaw, testament confirmed on
> 12 November 1698.

*St. Andrews Commissariat Testaments, Index, 1549-1800* (Francis J. Grant, Edinburgh, 1902):

> William Guthrie, in the Grange of Conan, parish of St.
> Vigeans, testament confirmed, 25 July 1599; Isobel Pirie,
> relict of William Robertson a merchant in Arbroath,
> daughter of David Pirie a merchant in Johnshaven
> and Janet Chaplain both deceased, which last was
> sister-german of the also deceased George Chaplain of
> Jamaica, and James Chaplain of Colliston in the parish of
> Arbroath, testament confirmed on 29 March 1775; David
> Wardlaw of Nether Beith, a merchant in Dunfermline,
> testament confirmed on 20 December 1791.

*Shetland Commissariat Testaments, Index, 1611-1650* (Edinburgh, 1904):

> Synnevo Paulsdochter, spouse to Gotherum Lundyman
> in Funze, Isle of Fetlar, testament confirmed on 24 July
> 1615; Erasmus Olason, in Collasetter, Isle of Unst,
> testament confirmed on 4 July 1631.

*Stirling Commissariat Testaments, Index, 1607-1800* (Francis J. Grant, Edinburgh, 1904)

> Lodowick Murray, a gunner in His Majesty's Castle of
> Stirling, testament confirmed on 31 May 1759; Alexander

Bowie, a merchant in Clackmannan and Margaret Burn his
spouse, testament confirmed on 13 February 1733; Henry
Rue, carpenter on board the ship *Eliza* trading from the
Clyde to the West Indies, son of the deceased Adam Rue in
St. Ninians, testament confirmed, 6 September 1782.

*Wigtown Commissariat Testaments, Index, 1700-1800* (Francis J. Grant,
Edinburgh, 1902):

John Todd, sometime a hardware merchant in Belfast,
now in Wigtown, testament confirmed in 1713; Captain
James Maxwell in Newton Stewart, second son of the
deceased Sir Alexander Maxwell of Monreith and his
spouse Elizabeth Maxwell, testament confirmed in 1798.

# OTHER COURT RECORDS

The old Royal Burghs had Burgh Courts, which tried offences that occurred within the burgh.

**Publications**. *The Burgh Court Book of Selkirk, 1503-1545* (John Imrie,
Edinburgh, 1960); *The Court Book of Kirkintilloch, 1658-1694* (George
S. Pryde, Edinburgh 1963; *The Court Book of Shetland, 1602-1604* (Gor-
don Donaldson, Edinburgh, 1954); *The Records of the Justiciary Court of
Edinburgh, 1661-1678*, two parts (W. G. Scott-Moncrieff, Edinburgh,
1905); *The Justiciary Records of Argyll and the Isles* (Edinburgh, 1959);
*The Gild Court Book of Dunfermline, 1433-1597* (Elizabeth P. D. Torrie,
Edinburgh, 1986); *The Lochmaben Court and Council Book, 1612-1721*
(J. B. Wilson, Edinburgh, 2001); *Court Minutes of Balgair, from 1706 to
1736* (Jean Dunlop, Edinburgh, 1957).

*Scottish American Court Records, from 1733 to 1783* (David Dobson,
Baltimore, 1991) contains brief abstracts of court cases involving people
linked to others on opposite sides of the Atlantic, for example:

On 4 August 1775, John McLeod, a missionary from
Harris in the Hebrides, later in Anson County, North
Carolina, John Grant of Pitkerrald, in Urquhart, Inverness-
shire, Ninian Menzies a Scottish merchant in Richmond,
Virginia, and others, versus David Ross, an accountant in

Edinburgh, the trustee of McPherson and Grant merchants
in Edinburgh (NRS.CS16.I.165).

***Records in Archives***. Some of the Burgh Court records are in the NRS
and others in local archives. The Records of the Burgh Court of Irvine
from 1604 to 1866 (AYA. IB2/1 and IB1/E) and those of Kilmarnock
from 1656 to 1796 (AYA.BK1.1.1) are in the Ayrshire Archives. Seri-
ous cases, such as major assault and robbery, were dealt with by Sheriff
Courts, the records of which are in the NRS (NRS.SC45).

The Court of Session deals with divorce, breach of contract, bankrupt-
cy, and more. Its records are also in the NRS (NRS.CS.). The Court of
Session contains several cases with transatlantic connections, for example
those of Adam Christie junior, a merchant in Pensacola; Alexander and
Mitchell, merchants in Antigua; William McCaa, a merchant in Virginia;
John Parker junior, a merchant in Kingston, Jamaica; John Crichton,
mate of the Dolphin of Glasgow; and John Cramond, a merchant in
Norfolk, Virginia, versus Patrick Telfer, a merchant in Glasgow, on 25
February 1778 (NRS.CS16.1.173).

The Lerwick, Shetland, Court books from the fifteenth to the twentieth
century are in the National Records of Scotland (NRS.SC12). Edinburgh
City Archives has the records of the Edinburgh Burgh Court from 1507
to 1828 (ECA.SL.233-234); the records of the Leith Burgh Court from
1624 to1920 (ECA.SL.86); and the records of Queensferry Burgh Court
from 1661 to 1966 (ECA.SL.59).

## MARITIME RECORDS

Seafaring was, and continues to be, of importance to an island nation
such as the United Kingdom. When you consider the relevance of seafaring to Scottish society and the economy over the centuries, it does
not seem improbable that at least some of our ancestors were engaged
in that industry. The likelihood increases when you take into account
that the majority of Scotland's population has traditionally lived in close
proximity to the sea. Having established a maritime connection, where
does the researcher turn next?

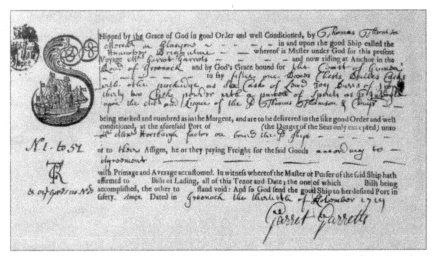

Shipping document, a rare piece of evidence to Scotland's small-scale involvement in the slave trade *(courtesy of National Records of Scotland)*

**Publications.** Possibly the best single source, especially if the ancestor lived in the Victorian era, is the Society of Genealogists' *My Ancestor Was a Merchant Seaman. How can I find out more about him?* (C. and M. Watts, London 1991), especially for the nineteenth century. However, the emphasis there is on English records, which may contain references to Scottish ships and seamen. Another great source is Eric J. Graham's *A Maritime History of Scotland, 1650-1790* (East Linton, 2002).

A book concentrating on Scottish sources and an earlier period is *Scottish Maritime Records, 1600-1850* (David Dobson, Baltimore, 1997). For centuries the monopoly of foreign trade in Scotland was in the hands of the Royal Burghs and their ports. Only they could engage in international commerce and much of the coastal trade. Until the rise of transatlantic trade in the late seventeenth century, the emphasis of foreign trade lay between east-coast ports—especially Leith, Dundee, and Aberdeen—and ports in Scandinavia, along the Baltic, and the Netherlands, while west-coast ports such as Glasgow and Ayr traded with Ireland, western England, France, and Iberia. The political union of Scotland and England in 1707 enabled Scottish ports such as Greenock and Glasgow to participate freely in transatlantic trade, to the comparative decline of the east-coast trade.

The records of the Customs and Excise, the department responsible for recording exports and imports and the port books, are best described in Frances Wilkins' books *Scottish Customs and Excise Records, with particular reference to Strathclyde, from 1707 onwards* (Widderminster, 1992) and her *Family Histories in Scottish Customs Records* (Wyre Forest, 1992). Local authorities also have records relating to shipping, some of which are in print, such as *Aberdeen Shore Works, 1596-1670*, but most are still in their original manuscript form, such as "The Shoremasters Account Book of Dundee, 1753-1800."

James T. Davidson provides useful insight into the contents and operation of a seamen's society in his *The Prime Gilt Box of Kirkcaldy* (1946). While that society dates from the late sixteenth century, the earliest surviving manuscript records commence in 1612. Davidson concentrates in his book on the period 1612 to 1674 and deals with topics such as the meaning of prime gilt, the origins of the society, its lands and heritages, the dangers of piracy, prisoners of war, voyages, shipwrecked sailors, burials, and various other subjects.

Publications about maritime records include *Admiralty Court Book of Scotland, 1557-1562* (T. C. Wade, Stair Society, Edinburgh, 1937), which records the proceedings of the High Court of the Admiralty of Scotland in the middle of the sixteenth century. One case before the court in 1560 involved the earliest-known vessel from the Americas arriving in Scotland, though not arriving as originally planned:

> On 7 December 1560 "Johne Schothart," a Frenchman, master of the *Francis of St. Martins* on the Isle du Rhe, claimed that he was returning from Newfoundland with his children and company as well as cargo, when attacked and captured by John Whitehead, master of an English ship *The Antelope* off the coast of Normandy, who then took the ship with its cargo to Dundee.

There has been an Admiralty Court in Scotland since the fifteenth century, though the records only date from 1557. The records of the court have been deposited with the National Records of Scotland in Edinburgh. This source has been little used by family historians. Using the records can be challenging and time-consuming, but fortunately maritime historians Eric J. Graham and Sue Mowat have produced a series of abstracts from the records, published in a CD entitled *High Court of the Admiralty of Scotland Records, 1627-1750*, which contains much information of use to the family historian. The following extract identifies an apprentice weaver from Paisley, an early textile town, who had absconded to be a recruit for a regiment in Dutch service, an option taken up by thousands of young Scots for around two hundred years.

> AC10/325 Petition for John Gilmour weaver of Paisley,
> and Andrew Sheilds of Marchstanehouse—1747. For
> a warrant to search a ship in Leith Roads, master ....
> Duncan, bound for Holland, and to arrest John Sheilds,
> son of Andrew and apprentice to Gilmour. John Sheilds
> has been recruited at Glasgow by sergeant Stewart to serve
> in General Colyer's Regiment in the service of the Estates
> General (of Holland). Enclosed: Warrant and Declaration!

Another option for consulting Admiralty Court records is the book *American Data from the Records of the High Court of the Admiralty of Scotland, 1675-1800* (David Dobson, Baltimore, 2000). It covers a slightly different period and concentrates on abstracts with some transatlantic link. It includes abstracts of Admiralty Court cases, such as the following:

> 19 December 1788 involving John Alston junior, a
> merchant in Glasgow, who sued Duncan Smith, a ship
> carpenter in Greenock, and owner of the brigantine
> *Elizabeth and Thomas*. The case concerned money given
> on 5 November 1787 by Robert Liddell of Baltimore,
> Maryland, to Thomas Adair, master of the *Elizabeth and
> Thomas* to be delivered on arrival in Glasgow to Walter
> Ewing, a merchant there. The money comprised of 220
> new dollars, 138 old dollars, 97 French half crowns, 150
> English shillings, and a half Johannes, 72 English guineas,
> and 17 English half-guineas (NRS.AC7.63).

Many of the actions before the Admiralty Court pertained to trade:

> June 21, 1782. Andrew Thomson, a merchant in Glasgow,
> versus William Snodgrass, sometime merchant in Glasgow
> now in North America, for money owing as a partner of a

> business. Andrew Thomson, William Snodgrass, George
> McCall, merchants in Glasgow, with Archibald Bryce
> and John Snodgrass, merchants in Virginia, formed a
> partnership on 25 February 1778 for carrying on trade in
> stores in Richmond and in Goochland, Virginia (NRS.
> AC7.58).

Other publications include "Papers of a Dundee Shipping Dispute, 1600-1604" by W.A. McNeill, in *Miscellany of the Scottish History Society Publications*, Volume X, which deals with a court case of a Dundee ship trading between Newfoundland and Portugal; *A Short History of the Shipmasters' Society of Aberdeen, 1598-1911* (Alexander Clark, Aberdeen, 1911); *Dumfries and Galloway Smuggling Story* (Frances Wilkins, Wyre Forest, 1993); *The Smuggling Story of Two Firths* (Frances Wilkins, Wyre Forest, 1995), which deals with smugglers operating off the Firths of Tay and Forth, based largely on Customs records; *The Smugglers* (Duncan Fraser, Montrose, 1971); *Maritime Scotland* (Brian Lavery, London, 2001); and *Scottish Seafarers of the Seventeenth Century* (David Dobson, Edinburgh, 1992).

An example of a listing from David Dobson's *Scottish Seafarers of the Eighteenth Century* (Edinburgh, 1996) follows:

> Henry Sinclair, son of Magnus Sinclair, of the merchant
> ship 'Wentworth' who died in Boston, New England,
> probate, February 1777, Prerogative Court of Canterbury.

*Scottish Seafarers from 1800 to 1830* (David Dobson, St. Andrews, 1997) lists mariners for whom there are wills or testaments, mainly in Scotland and the Prerogative Court of Canterbury. Dobson also published the following series of maritime source books identifying seafarers: *The Mariners of St. Andrews and the East Neuk of Fife, from 1600 to 1700* (St. Andrews, 1992); *The Mariners of Kirkcaldy and West Fife, from 1600 to 1700* (St. Andrews, 1992); *The Mariners of Fife, from 1700 to 1800* (1994); *The Mariners of the Clyde and Western Scotland, from 1600 to 1700* (St. Andrews, 1994); *The Mariners of the Clyde and Western Scotland from 1700 to 1800*, two parts (St. Andrews, 1994, 1999); *The Mariners of the Lothians, from 1700 to 1800* (St. Andrews, 1995); *The Mariners of the Lothians from 1600 to 1700*, two parts (St. Andrews, 1993); *The Mar-*

*iners of Aberdeen and Northern Scotland, from 1600 to 1700* (St. Andrews, 1993); *The Mariners of Aberdeen and Northern Scotland, from 1700 to 1800*, two parts (St. Andrews, 1994, 1997); *The Mariners of Angus, from 1600 to 1700* (St. Andrews,1992); *The Mariners of Angus, from 1700 to 1800*, two parts (St. Andrews, 1993, 1995); *A Directory of Seafarers of the East Neuk of Fife from 1580 to 1800* (St. Andrews, 2008); *Aberdeen Shipping from 1742 to 1746: Ships, Shipmasters and Voyages* (St. Andrews, 2005); *Aberdeen Shipping, from 1746 to 1748: Ships, Shipmasters and Voyages* (St. Andrews, 2006); *Aberdeen Shipping, from 1748 to 1751: Ships, Shipmasters and Voyages* (St. Andrews, 2007); *Aberdeen Shipping, from 1751 to 1753: Ships, Shipmasters and Voyages* (St. Andrews, 2007); *The Shipping of Perth, from 1717 to 1767: Ships, Shipmasters and Voyages* (St. Andrews, 2005); *The Shipping of Anstruther and the East Neuk of Fife, from 1742 to 1771: Ships, Shipmasters and Voyages* (St. Andrews, 2008); *Dundee Shipping, from 1760 to 1769: Ships, Shipmasters and Voyages* (St. Andrews, 2005); *Dundee Shipping, from 1770 to 1784: Ships, Shipmasters and Voyages* (St. Andrews); *The Shipmasters of Dundee, from 1775 to 1825* (St. Andrews, 2006); *The Shipping of Dundee and Montrose from 1720 to 1750: Ships, Shipmasters and Voyages* (St. Andrews, 2005).

Other publications include *Ships from Scotland to Australasia, from 1820 to 1860* (David Dobson, Milbury, South Australia, 2005); *Ships from Scotland to America, from 1628 to 1828*, four volumes (David Dobson, Baltimore, 1998-2011); *Ships from Scotland to North America, 1830-1860*, two volumes (Baltimore, 2002, 2008); *The Terror of the Seas? Scottish Maritime Warfare, 1513-1713* (Steve Murdoch, Boston and Leiden, 2010), which deals with privateers and pirates and war at sea in the sixteenth and seventeenth centuries.

The best single source on Dundee and its seafarers is Hamish Robertson's *Mariners of Dundee: Their City, Their River, Their Fraternity* (Dundee, 2006). Also check out *The Trade and Shipping of Dundee, 1780-1850* (Gordon Jackson, Dundee, 1991); *The Port of Leith* (Sue Mowat, Edinburgh, 1994); *The Port of Montrose* (Gordon Jackson and S. C. E. Lythe, Tayport, 1993); and *The Old Scots Navy* (J. Grant, London, 1914).

***Records in Archives.*** Scottish port books can be used to identify the ships, shipmasters, and merchants participating in international trade. Found in the NRS, these are incomplete for the seventeenth century (NRS.E71-E72, series) but comprehensive from 1742 to 1828 (NRS. E504, series). While the shipmasters are relatively well recorded, crew members and passengers are not. The port books from 1828 are in the National Archives in London.

Every port of any consequence had a mariners' or seamen's society operating for the collective use of its members. Their records were contained is what is known as Sea Boxes. Before the start of a voyage, each crew member subscribed to a fund, out of which his dependents would receive a pension if he was lost at sea; it also would help support him during illness or old-age. The voyages and vessels of the seamen can be traced through the records contained in the Sea Box. Many of these Sea Boxes have survived in local archives or libraries. The Sea Box of Bo'ness, 1634 to 1984, now with the National Library of Scotland in Edinburgh (NLS. Deposit 259), contains references to skippers and seamen. For example,

> on 21 October 1743, Helen Kidd, widow of Andrew
> Air, a sailor of Bo'ness, who had failed to return from a
> voyage, was granted one pound and sixteen shillings.

The Perth and Kinross Archives holds the records of the Perth Merchant Seamans' Fund. Sea Boxes survive for other ports, such as Anstruther from 1737 to 1943 (NRS.B3.7.3); Pittenweem from 1633 to 1757, and from 1787 to 1840 (NRS.B3.7.4/5); and St. Monance for 1834 (NRS. FS1.11.28). Probably the only book in print is that of Aberdeen, within *A Short History of the Shipmasters' Society of Aberdeen 1598-1911* (A. Clark, Aberdeen, 1911).

From 1835 it has been compulsory to have crew lists; the NRS has some, while the Glasgow City Archives has crew lists for vessels owned by Hugh Hogarth between 1861 and 1890 (GCA.TD816.37). Merchant Navy crew lists exist from 1861 to 1913, and some from 1835, in local record offices, but most are now in the Maritime History Archive in Newfoundland. The NRS has whaling and herring fishery bounties, which list the crew by name, age, place of residence, and occupation. Examples of the information in these records are as follows:

> Normand McLeod, born 1751 in Barvas, a crewman
> aboard the herring buss, the *Barbara of Stornaway*, in
> 1777 (NRS.E508.76.9.158)

and

> Donald McKay, born 1733 in Bowmore, a mariner in
> Islay, co-owner of the herring buss *Flora of Islay* in 1777
> (NRS.E505.76.9.11).

Records pertaining to the Seamen's Box of Aberdeen *(courtesy of the Aberdeen Maritime Museum)*

The Dundee City Archives has the records of the Fraternity of Seamen of Trinity House, Dundee, which date from the middle of the seventeenth century, though the majority are from the nineteenth century. The earliest surviving documents are the Boxmaster's Accounts for the period 1652 to 1695, which include the admission of new members and the election of boxmasters. The next group of manuscripts are the "Index of Masters, from 1785 to 1861," which records admissions to the Fraternity (DCA. GD/Hu/SF/10/1), and the "Index of Mates and Seamen, from 1799 to 1859," which records dates of admission to the Fraternity (DCA.GD/Hu/ HF/10/2). There are also pension lists from 1851 to 1943 for Masters, their widows, and children (DCA.GD/Hu/HF/11/1-3, and 12/2). "The Fraternity of Masters and Seamen of Trinity House in Dundee," Frank Mudie, ms. 1962 (DCA.GD/Hu/SF/22/7), is an unpublished history. The records of the Kincardine Seamen and Sailors Friendly Society, from 1744 to 1821, can be consulted in the Stirling Archives.

Apprentice seafarers also had indentureship deeds, which were registered in sources such as the local Register of Deeds. Below is an example from the Dundee Burgh Register of Deeds:

> At Dundee, 25 March 1752, it is agreed between John
> Auchenleck, shipmaster in Dundee, on the one part
> and Alexander Jarron, lawful son to the deceased David
> Jarron in Carmyllie, with the consent of William Jarron,
> a cowfeeder in Dundee, and James Husband, maltman
> there, his cautioners, . . . that Alexander Jarron becomes
> and binds himself apprentice to and with the daid John
> Auchenleck for learning of and serving him in the sailor's
> art or calling and that for the full space of five years from
> the date hereof . . .

Inverkeithing Burgh Records contain indenture listings such as the following:

> Charles Wilson in Inverkeithing, son of Charles Wilson,
> carpenter presently abroad, was apprenticed to William
> Walker, tenant in Orchardhead, and John Walker in
> Inverkeithing, owners of the sloop *The Six Sisters of
> Inverkeithing* in the navigation and seafaring business for
> three years from 17 March 1812.

Indenture agreement *(courtesy of National Records of Scotland)*

The use of sources such as the Register of Deeds can be rewarding but sometimes quite challenging due to the script in the early sources, but some volumes are well indexed, which facilitates research. This indexation has been thoroughly done for the Registers of Deeds of the Council of Session held in the National Records of Scotland, while the local Registers of Deeds held in archives throughout Scotland are only partially indexed.

Local newspapers—such as the *Aberdeen Journal*, dating from 1747—regularly carried reports on shipping, particularly those pertaining to the north east of Scotland. Leith Commercial Lists are particularly good on shipping in the Victorian era, as was the "Naval Intelligence" column of *The Scotsman*.

## FISHING

Fishing has long been an important industry in Scotland, employing thousands of men and women, so there is a reasonable chance that there may be fishing ancestors in the family. The Royal Fishing Company, which encouraged the development of the herring fishery, was established in 1677, with its main base in Greenock on the Clyde. Possibly the earliest collection of documents dealing with fishermen are the Records of the Society of Free Fishermen of Newhaven on the Forth, dating between 1572 and 1935. These documents have been deposited with the National Records of Scotland in Edinburgh. One of the early documents is a letter dated 30 May 1625:

> . . . raised at the instance of Robert Or, indweller (resident) in Newheavin, Helen Wilsoun his spouse, and Thomas Robesoun his son-in-law, against Norman Hunter, fisher, indweller in Newheavin, Isabel Wallis his spouse, Gilbert Hunter his brother in law, and Thomas Glassfurd, servant to the said Norman (NRS.GD265.4.1.3).

From the mid-eighteenth century onward, the British government again began to provide support for the fishing industry, especially herring fishing, for example with bounties paid between 1752 and 1796 to encourage its growth. From the surviving records, now in the NRS, it is possible to identify skippers, crews, and their vessels. These records of bounties paid are well detailed, giving the names, ages, places of residence, and ages of the skippers and crewmen. The documents (NRS.E508) are particularly useful in areas such as the Hebrides where genealogical records are less common. Take, for example, the herring bounty paid in 1794 to John McIvor, crewman aboard the herring buss *Providence of Stornaway*, who was born in Stornaway in 1770, or to William McDonald, born 1757, a crewman aboard the herring buss *Janet of Stornaway* in 1777.

In 1785 the British Fisheries Society was founded with the aim of developing the infrastructure of the industry, such as the construction and restoration of harbors and "fishertouns," such as Ullapool in Wester Ross and at Pultneytown near Wick in Caithness. The Society's records are in the NRS. In 1808 an Act for the further encouragement and better regulation of the Scottish herring industry was passed. The Records of the Scottish Fishery Board (NRS.AF.1.38) date from 1809 and contain correspondence with, and regarding, fishermen; for example, a letter of 1836 about Donald McGrigor, a fisherman on the Isle of Tanera, regarding money to be shared with Robert McLeod for the building of a new boat states, "they are both very poor men, each having a wife and eight children to support."

Local libraries and museums often contain unique source material. The Scottish Fisheries Museum at Crail has a three-volume typescript work entitled "Anecdotes of Fish and Fishermen in the East Neuk of Fife, 1452 -1955" and a range of books, including *A Directory of Seafarers of the East Neuk of Fife, 1580-1800* (St. Andrews, 2008) and *Crail and Its Fisheries, 1550-1600* (Thomas Riis, St. Andrews, 2016), the history of a community heavily dependent on the fishing industry, listing many of the participants, their ships, and fishing grounds.

Other publications about the fishing industry include *The Society of Free Fishermen of Newhaven* (James Wilson, Newhaven, 1951); and *The British Fisheries Society, 1786-1893* (Jean Dunlop, Edinburgh, 1978).

## WHALING

Closely connected to the fishing industry was whaling. While there were attempts to establish a whaling industry in the seventeenth century, it did not become successful until the mid-eighteenth century. In 1733 the British government began to offer bounties on whaling. This attracted English seafarers to engage in whaling, but it was not until 1749 that Scottish companies became involved. Within a few years the Edinburgh Whale Fishing Company, the Aberdeen Whale Fishing Company, and the Dundee Whale Fishing Company were established.

A Parliamentary Report claimed that between 1750 and 1786 around 367 whaling voyages from Scotland to Greenland and to the Davis Straits had occurred. The skippers and crews were, at first, recruited from the ranks, though some of the harpooners appear to have been Dutch or Scandinavian. By the late eighteenth century, the average crew of a whaling ship consisted of the master, the mate, a surgeon, six harpooners, six steersmen, six line managers, six landsmen alias greenmen, six apprentices, and seventeen sailors. Here again the records of bounties paid are very useful, as they provide the names and occupation of every member of the crew. For example, the records show that William Smith was steersman aboard the *Satisfaction of Greenock*, which whaled off Greenland in 1786 (NRS.E508.84.8.12), while James Anderson was harpooner aboard the *Tay of Dundee*, whaling in the Davis Strait in 1813 (NRS.E508. 115.8). The whaling bounty documents, like the herring bounty, are all original documents, boxed according to year and bundled within the boxes according to the port of record. These ports were mainly on the east coast from Dunbar, north to Peterhead, with Glasgow, Greenock, and Campbeltown on the west coast.

Contemporary newspapers can be a source of genealogical facts concerning shipping. For example, the *Aberdeen Journal* of 7 April 1813 reported the loss of the whaling ship *Oscar of Aberdeen* in Aberdeen Bay a few days earlier, when 44 members of the crew perished and only two survived. The deceased were mostly from Aberdeen or nearby, apart from three from England. Some were buried in nearby graveyards; an epitaph in Newburgh churchyard has the following inscription:

> Sacred to the memory of Captain John Innes, aged 42 years,
> who was wrecked in the ship *Oscar*, near Aberdeen, the 1st
> April 1813. This stone is erected by his disconsolate widow,
> Ann Mitchell, as a grateful tribute of her regard and affection
> for his departed worth. Their son, Thomas, who died in
> infancy, is also interred here. Also his spouse, Ann Mitchell,
> died 16th November 1828, aged 68 years.

This provides useful genealogical data. Since the Mitchells were buried in the Newburgh churchyard, they were presumably Presbyterians, members of the parish church. They possibly baptized their son there, perhaps originated there, information that the Old Parish Registers of baptism and marriage may confirm.

There are several books available that deal with Scotland and whaling. A recent one is *The Dundee Whaling Fleet: Ships, Masters and Men*, which lives up to its title: Especially of interest to the family historian is Appendix 3, which identifies many of the men who sailed aboard Dundee whalers, their occupation aboard ship, the name of the ship, the year, and miscellaneous notes. For example, it tells us that Alexander Allan, aged 25, born in Peterhead, was sail-maker and boat steerer aboard the *Diana* on her voyage to Antarctica in 1892-1893. A chapter on Dundee Ship Masters provides much more detail on the skippers of Dundee ships. Dundee University Archives has the papers of two local companies, the Dorothy Whale Fishing Company and the Friendship Whale Fishing Company, from 1829 to 1837, as well as substantial material on the Tay Whaling Company, dating from 1791, which includes details of voyages, ships, catches, skippers, and crews.

Some publications dealing with whaling and listing the crews include David Dobson's *The Whalers of Dundee, 1750-1850* (St. Andrews, 1995) and his *Scottish Whalers before 1800* (St. Andrews, 1995). Other publications of interest include *Whaling and the Hebrides* (John Baldwin, Canterbury 2008); *The Arctic Whalers* (Basil Lubbock, Glasgow, 1955); *Whalehunters: Dundee and the Arctic Whalers* (Malcolm Archibald, Edinburgh, 2004), which has crew lists for 1808 to 1815; *The Dundee Whalers* (Norman Watson, East Linton, 2003); *The Whale Hunters* (Robert Smith, Edinburgh, 1993); *Captain James Fairweather, Whaler and Shipmaster: His Life and Career 1853-1933* (Nancy Rycroft, Ripponden, 2005); and *Whales and Whaling* (Arthur G. Credland, Aylesbury, 1982).

## BURGH RECORDS

Burghs were established in Scotland from the mid-thirteenth century onward—the first being Berwick-on-Tweed, then within the borders of Scotland. A burgh was a semi-autonomous community, usually a market town or port, which was granted a Royal Charter incorporating it with special privileges. Burghs were under the control of town or burgh councils, which were elected from within the ranks of the local merchant and craftsmen who formed the burgesses.

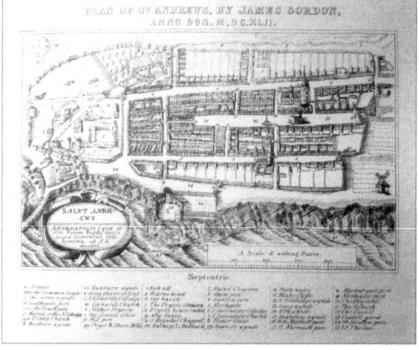

Map of 17th-century St. Andrews *(courtesy of the University of St. Andrews)*

The burgesses were a self-perpetuating group, usually less than ten percent of the male residents. To become a burgess a man had to meet one or more of the following criteria: have served an apprenticeship under an existing burgess, be the son of a burgess, or have married the daughter of a burgess, with a few being admitted on payment of a fee or in appreciation of some service to the community. The latter option occurred when someone made a special effort in the defense of the burgh (for example, Alexander Air, a smith in Leith, was admitted as a burgess of Edinburgh in 1669 for service as a corporal of Captain Oliphant's militia in Leith). Some Loyalists and soldiers who had returned from America were admitted as burgesses—men such as Donald McDonald, a former Lieutenant of the North Carolina Highlanders, in 1789, and Captain John Peebles, late of the 42nd (Black Watch) Regiment of Foot, in 1786, were admitted as burgesses of Ayr. On occasion, a former resident who was based abroad at the time was admitted as a burgess of his hometown, partly to commemorate his success but mainly for economic reasons. As a burgess he would be able to trade in his hometown without restriction and so stimulate trade between his place of origin and his place of residence. An example was the case of Robert Stewart, a factor in Bordeaux, who was admitted as a burgess and guilds-brother of Ayr in 1673.

Burgesses were members of the relevant crafts or merchant guilds, which supervised the training of apprentices, maintained the standards of work, and also protected the interests of members. It was, therefore, essential that records of burgesses, as well as those of the trades and merchants, especially apprenticeships, be maintained. The records of the admission of burgesses and of the burgh councils should exist in burgh archives and sometimes in print in local libraries throughout Scotland. The Scottish Archive Network (SCAN) is in the process of compiling information about Scottish burghs and where historical records relating to burghs can be found (**https://www.scan.org.uk/familyhistory/ myancestor/burgess.htm**).

The work of the Scottish Record Society (**www.scottishre- cordsociety.org.uk/**) also comes in useful. Among their publications are *Roll of Edinburgh Burgesses, 1406-1841*, in four volumes; *Burgesses and Guild Brethren of Glasgow, 1751-1846*; *Roll of Dunbarton Burgesses and Guild Brethren, 1600-1846*; and *Register of the Burgesses of the Canongate, 1622-1733*. The published versions are available in most reference libraries in Scotland and on the Scottish Record Society website. The following is an example of what you'll find on the Glasgow burgess roll lists:

> Patrick Laing, a baker, who having served his
> apprenticeship under John Garner, a baker in Glasgow,
> was then admitted to the Baker Incorporation of
> Glasgow and in 1739 as a burgess and guilds-brother
> there in 1739.

The Reform Act of 1832 withdrew many of the privileges held by burgesses and increased the franchise. Formerly, only burgesses could vote in council elections or operate businesses within the burgh boundaries. As becoming a burgess was the way to social and economic success in the burgh, it was essential that records were maintained by the burgh as well as by the crafts or trades and merchant guilds. Such records sometimes date back to the medieval period and are a potential treasure trove for family historians.

A good introduction to life in a Scottish burgh is Craig Mair's *Mercat Cross and Tolbooth* (Edinburgh, 1988); another is Michael Lynch's *The Early Modern Town in Scotland* (Wolfeboro, 1987), as well as Derek Hall's *Burgess, Merchant and Priest. Burgh Life in the Scottish Medieval Town* (Edinburgh, 2002). Edinburgh City Archives has the records of Edinburgh and Leith from 1639 to 1920 (ECA.SL224) as well as the records of the Royal Burgh of Queensferry from 1634 to 1975 (ECA.SL59). It also contains the registers of voters in Edinburgh from 1832 to 1974 (ECA.SL56).

Some of the Scottish family history societies and antiquarian societies, such as the Spalding Society in Aberdeen, have published various local records, including burgess rolls. In 2002 the Ayrshire Federation of Historical Societies published *The Burgesses and Guild Brethren of Ayr, 1647-1846*. Ayr, a west-coast port, had important trading links with Ireland and the colonies from the seventeenth century onward. An excerpt from the book states that "on 8 July 1656 Mr James Gordon, minister at Cumber, was admitted as a burgess and guilds-brother of Ayr by the right of Elizabeth Gordon his wife, eldest lawful daughter of Robert Gordon the late Provost." This tells the researcher that James Gordon had settled in Ireland during the Plantation of Ulster; that he was a minister, highly likely to have been a Presbyterian; and that the title "Mr" implies that he was a graduate, possibly of Glasgow, the nearest university, which suggests a search of that university's matriculation and graduation lists, as well as a search of the *Fasti Ecclesiae Scoticanae*, which provides biographical data on Church of Scotland ministers since the Reformation of 1560. James had been eligible to be a burgess of Ayr by right of his wife, who was a daughter of the provost of Ayr (the provost is the chief magistrate of all Scottish burghs and automatically a burgess).

Burgess Rolls publications by David Dobson include *The Burgess Rolls of Fife, 1700-1800*, two volumes (St. Andrews, 1994/1996); *The Burgesses of Perth, from 1600 to 1699* (St. Andrews, 2002); and *The Burgess Roll of St. Andrews, 1700-1775*, two volumes (David Dobson, St. Andrews, 1994/1995).

The following is an example of a listing from *The Burgesses and Guild Brethren of Ayr, 1647-1846* (A. Lindsay and J. Kennedy, Ayr, 2002):

> Mr John Campbell, minister of Rapho in Ireland, was admitted as a burgess and guilds brother of Ayr on 14 June 1658 by right of his wife Elizabeth Birnie, eldest daughter of John Birnie a burgess and guilds-brother, OR, Colonel Alexander McKenzie of Elizabeth City, Virginia, was admitted as a burgess and guilds-brother of Ayr on 25 March 1729.

Burgesses and guild brethren of Ayr *(courtesy of the Ayrshire Archaeological & Natural History Society)*

Publications by Frances J. McDonnell include *Register of Merchant and Trade Burgesses of Aberdeen, 1600-1620* (St. Andrews, 1994); *Register of Merchant and Trade Burgesses of Aberdeen, 1621-1639* (St. Andrews, 1994); *Register of Merchant and Trade Burgesses of Aberdeen 1640-1659* (St. Andrews, 1994); *Register of Merchant and Trade Burgesses of Aberdeen 1660-1679* (St. Andrews, 1994), an example from which is "On 22 November 1676, William MacLeod, a mason in the burgh, was licensed to brew and sell ale, beer, and aquavita, during all the days of his lifetime"; *The Burgess Rolls of Banff* (St. Andrews, 1994); *The Burgess Roll of Elgin* (St. Andrews, 1996); and *Merchants and Trade Burgesses of Old Aberdeen, 1605-1885* (St. Andrews, 2001).

---

### BURGESS ROLL OF ELGIN

No formal roll or book of burgesses having been kept, this list, consisting mainly of honorary burgesses, has been compiled from the Burgh and Court Books, tavern and other bills, and other sources, and is admittedly imperfect

**A**

Abbot, Captain          1786 "who belongs to Lossiemouth"

Adam, Alexander          1756, chapman in Unthank of Urquhart, "in consequence of the powers vested in the Provost of this burgh"

Adam, John          1637

Adam, William          1761, in Newmiln, "at desire of Provost Robertson"

Adam, William          1774, chapman, "out of the regard the magistrates bear to William Adam, merchant, late of the Town Council"

Alan, Benjamin          1709, servant to my Lord Grange

Allan, Alexander, jr          1751, merchant, Garmouth, "at the special desire and request of John Duff, late Provost"

Allan, Alexander          1775, son to Robert Allan, merchant

Allan, James          1774, "in Main, at desire of Alexander Brodie of Windyhills, late Provost"

Alves, Alexander          21 Sep 1765, son of Alexander Alves, farmer, "on account of the singular service done by him in extinguishing a fire which happened in this burgh lately in William Baird's houses"

Alves, John          1775, servant to Baillie Leslie, "at the desire of Patrick Duff, Town Clerk, and others to encourage qualified mechanics to reside in the place"

Anderson, Alexander          1774, shoemaker, "at the request of the Provost and others"

Anderson, Andrew          27 Feb 1644

Anderson, James          1723, brasier

---

Burgess Roll of Elgin *(courtesy of F. J. McDonnell)*

*The Roll of Canongate Burgesses, 1622-1733* (Helen Armit, Edinburgh, 1951) is particularly interesting because the burgh of Canongate, being close to Holyrood House and Parliament, attracted people of influence, landowners, merchants, and craftsmen, including a number of skilled immigrants such as Huguenot "Anthony Leureaux, a felt-maker, apprentice to Isaac Falcon a feltmaker," who was admitted as a burgess on 17 September, 1703, and "Francis Van Gent, a stamper, who was admitted as a burgess on the recommendation of Sir James Stewart, H.M. Advocate, on 26 August 1702."

*The Burgesses of Inveraray, 1665-1963* (E. Beaton and S. W. MacIntyre, Edinburgh, 1990) includes "James Boswell, the younger of Auchenleck, an advocate, on 6 September 1766; and Zachary McAulay, a merchant in Quebec, on 17 February 1767." Other publications include *Register of the Burgesses of the Burgh of the Canongate, 1622-1733* (H. Armet, SRS, Edinburgh, 1951); *The Burgesses and Guild-brothers of Glasgow, 1573-1846* (J. R. Anderson, SRS, Edinburgh, 1935); and *Roll of Dumbarton Burgesses and Guild-Brethren, from 1600 to 1846* (Fergus Roberts, Edinburgh, 1937).

**Records in Archives.** Glasgow City Archives has the Register of Burgesses of Glasgow from 1573 until 1969 (GCA.C5.1), which contains listings such as "Burgess ticket for John Gilmour, mason, as having married Jean, daughter of Ninian Crawford, a cordiner burgess, 20 September 1770" (GCA.TD200.76). Also in the Glasgow City Archives is the Register of the Burgesses of Rutherglen from 1620 to 1975 (GCA.RU3.5).

Fife Archives has a list of the Heritors and Burgesses of Leslie in 1755 (FA.B.Les.5.54); also the Register of Admission of Burgesses of Kirkcaldy from 1810 to 1965 (FA.B.KDY.12.1.8). Since the introduction of the Reform Act of 1832, the franchise was gradually expanded and electoral registers were kept that listed names, property owned, and occupations. For example, the Register of Voters in North Berwick, 1838 (NRS.B56.12.2) lists "Alec Maxwell Adams, a surgeon, George Begbie, a farmer, Peter Bertram, a baker."

# MERCHANTS

Economic and social power in the burghs was in the hands of the burgess-es during the medieval and early modern period. Merchants had to meet the same requirements as craftsmen to become burgesses as described above. They formed burghs' Merchant Gilds or Guilds, which date from the twelfth century, and were described as guild-brothers. Merchants, as burgesses, had trading rights not only within the burgh but also in a substantial surrounding area known as "the Liberties." Royal Burghs had a monopoly on overseas trade; for example, only the burgesses of Dundee could buy wool or skins within the sheriffdom of Forfar, and only they could trade with foreign merchants who came to Dundee.

**Publications.** *The Guildry of Dundee* (Annette M. Smith, Dundee, 2005), a history of the Merchant Guild of Dundee back to the medieval period; *The Company of Merchants of the City of Edinburgh, 1681-1981* (Nancy H. Miller, Edinburgh, 1981); *The Rise and Progress of the Company of Merchants of the City of Edinburgh, 1681-1902* (A. Heron, Edinburgh, 1903); *Fife Traders and Shopkeepers, 1820-1870*, ten volumes (Andrew Campbell, Kirkcaldy, 1989); *The Stirling Merchant Gild and the Life of John Cowan* (David B. Morris, Stirling, 1919); *Extracts from the Guildry Records of Stirling, 1592-1846* (W. B. Cook, Stirling, 1916); "Register of the Guild and Trade Burgesses of the Burgh of Aberdeen, from 1399 to 1631," in *Miscellany of the New Spalding Club, Volume I* (Aberdeen, 1890); *The Gild Court Book of Dunfermline from 1433 to 1597* (Elizabeth P. D. Torrie, Edinburgh, 1986); *The Court Books of Orkney and Shetland, from 1614 to 1615* (Robert S. Barclay, Edinburgh, 1967); *Aberdeen Gild Court Records, from 1437 to 1468* (E. Gemmill, Edinburgh, 2005); and *The Guildry of Edinburgh* (James Colston, Edinburgh, 1887).

*Scottish Transatlantic Merchants, from 1611 to 1785,* by David Dobson (Baltimore, 2007), contains listings such as the following

> Archibald Lundie, born 1750, a merchant from
> Edinburgh, who emigrated via Greenock to New York,
> settled in Savanna, Georgia, as a merchant, a Loyalist
> in 1776 who moved to St. Augustine, Florida, and later
> to the West Indies, and Alexander Spiers, born 1714, a

merchant who emigrated to Virginia in 1740, a planter
in Elderslie, a Loyalist who returned to Glasgow by 1781,
and died there in 1782.

***Records in Archives.*** Edinburgh City Archives has the Records of the
Merchant Company of Edinburgh from 1468 to 1989 (ECA.242),
which include the widows fund papers, hospital records, and educational
records; also the Records of the Society of High Constables from 1701
to 1985 (ECA.ED011). Glasgow City Archives has the Records of the
Merchant House of Glasgow, from 1558 to 1975 (GCA.T-MH), and
Stirling Archives has the Records of the Merchant Guildry of Stirling
from 1460 to 1988.

# CRAFTSMEN

If your ancestor had a particular trade, this could be extremely useful
for research purposes. Traditionally, all craftsmen served an apprenticeship under an existing qualified craftsman. Then, having satisfactorily
served a specified number of years, he became a journeyman qualified
to work at his trade. Every burgh had a craft or trade society that controlled the tradesmen of the burgh, set standards, overlooked apprentices,
and guarded the interests of the members. When the metal workers of
Glasgow petitioned in 1536 to establish an "Incorporation of Hammermen," they were protecting their members from competition from other
burghs. Trade or craft records generally have survived, some in the hands
of the craft, some in lawyers' offices, but mostly in local archives. They
are usually in original manuscripts; however, a few have been published,
including those of Edinburgh.

***Publications.*** Edinburgh, the biggest city, offered the widest range of
training opportunities, and so attracted apprentices from all over Scotland and elsewhere, including a few from the colonies. *The Register of
Apprentices of the City of Edinburgh*, though incomplete, has been published in three volumes for the period 1583 to 1800. It provides much
genealogical data—the name of the apprentice, the name of his father or
guardian and his occupation and place of residence, the name and trade
of the craftsman and his location, and the period of the apprenticeship.

## Register of Edinburgh Apprentices, 1666-1700.

Abercrombie, Alexr., s. to Thomas A., p. to James Wilsone, younger, mt.    13 June 1666
  ,,   James, s. to late Thomas A. in Leith, p. to Patrick Wat, mt.    13 Apr. 1670
  ,,   Patrick, s. to dec. Sir Alexr. A. of Birnboig, p. to James Nicolson of Trabrown, mt. (B.)    6 June 1694
Adam, George, s. to dec. John A., fermorer at Inglistoun, p. to Richard Brown, candlemaker (B.)    19 Apr. 1700
  ,,   Wm., s. to Wm. A., elder, mt. in Cullros, p. to John Cairns, stationer    27 Oct. 1680
  ,,   Wm., s. to dec. George A., tailor, p. to Andrew Powrie, apothecary (B.)    12 Jan. 1687
Adamson, Alexr., s. to Andrew A., indweller, p. to Archd. Hamiltoun, mt.    21 Apr. 1686
  ,,   Francis, s. to dec. James A. of Fleures, p. to John Armour, tailor (B.)    29 Mar. 1699
  ,,   James, s. to James A., customer at the west port, p. to James Padyeane, writer    29 Oct. 1673
  ,,   James, s. to umq. Andrew A., fermourer in Fordellmylne, p. to John Campbell, yer., tanner    1 Apr. 1685
  ,,   John, s. to Walter A. in Dalkeith, p. to John Adamson, baxter    28 Feb. 1666
  ,,   John, s. to Mr. John A., minr. of the gospel, p. to James Reid, mt.    9 July 1679
  =   John, s. to dec. James A., indweller, p. to Androw Nisbet, candlemaker    5 Sept. 1683
  ,,   John, s. to Alexr. A., indweller, p. to James Lenie, skinner    11 May 1687
  ,,   Patrick, s. to Patrick A., tenant to Alexr. Brand of Barbertoun, p. to John Lawder, coppersmith (B.)    13 Nov. 1695
  ,,   Robert, s. to Andrew A. in Fordellmill, p. to James Adamson, baxter. (*Defeit of consent*)    18 Aug. 1669
Adinstoa (Admiston), Lawrance, s. to Thomas A of Kirkcant, p. to John Nasmyth, wright    6 June 1688
  ,,   Wm., s. to Thomas A. of Carcant (Kirkcant), p. to Gavin Drysdaill, baxter    3 June 1674
Agnew, Alexr., s. to Alexr. A., indweller in Ireland, p. to Robert Selkirk, mt.    27 Aug. 1679
  ,,   Thomas, second s. to Sir Andrew A. of Lochnaw, p. to Robert Blackwood, mt.    23 Feb. 1687
Aikford, Robert, s. to late Thomas A. in Wormistoun, p. to John Loch, mt.    27 May 1674
Aikman, Andrew, s. to James A. in Williamston, p. to Robert Somervaill, skinner (B.)    6 Nov. 1696
  ,,   John, s. to John A. in Woodhouse of Calder, p. to Samuel Purdy, skinner    11 May 1681
  ,,   Wm., s. to John A. in the paroch of Crawmond, p. to John Shaw, baxter (B.)    1 Nov. 1693
Ainslie, Adam, s. to Wm. A., indweller, p. to John Blaiky, hatmaker    22 Aug. 1683

Register of Edinburgh apprentices *(courtesy of the Scottish Record Society)*

Take the case of George Seaman. The entry in the register reads, "Seaman, George, s. to Alexander S., baxter in Leith, p. to Charles Crockett, mt. (B), 1 Nov. 1721," which informs us that George, the son of a baker in Leith, the port of Edinburgh, served an apprenticeship to a merchant in

Edinburgh beginning in 1721. Further research reveals links with colonial Charleston, to which Charles Crockett traded, and where his son James Crockett settled. While George Seaman became a merchant burgess of Edinburgh, his kinsman George Seaman also settled in Charleston.

These published registers are generally available in university and local reference libraries throughout Scotland, and in digital form on the website of the Scottish Record Society (**www.scottishrecordsociety.org. uk/**). After a period of working as an apprentice, a craftsman could apply to become a burgess, which would enable him to conduct his own business within the burgh, employ journeymen, and train apprentices. As a burgess he had the right to vote in local elections, though the Reform Act of 1832 extended the right to other men in the burgh.

Other publications include *The Incorporated Trades of Edinburgh* (James Colston, Edinburgh, 1891), which deals with surgeons, wrights, goldsmiths, bakers, butchers, shoemakers, tailors, weavers, bonnet-makers, candlemakers and barbers; *The Records of the Trades House of Glasgow, 1713-1777* (Harry Lumsden, Glasgow, 1924), which contains substantial records on tradesmen in Glasgow during the eighteenth century, plus a history of the Trades House from 1605 to 1777; *History of the Incorporation of Cordiners in Glasgow* (William Campbell, Glasgow, 1883), which contains a list of deacons from 1758 to 1882, and a list of members and addresses from 1832 to 1883; *The Nine Incorporated Trades of Dundee* (Innes A. Duffus, Dundee, 2011), which is a concise history of the bakers, cordiners, glovers, tailors, bonnet-makers, fleshers, hammermen, weavers, and dyers of the burgh; *The Nine Trades of Dundee* (Annette M. Smith, Dundee, 1995); *The Brewers and Breweries of Stirlingshire* (Forbes Gibb, Stirling, 2008), which lists brewers from mid-eighteenth century; *The Shoemaker Incorporation of Perth, from 1545 to 1927* (Peter Baxter, Perth, 1927); *The Incorporation of Shoemakers of Stirling* (David B. Morris, Stirling, 1925); *Dunfermline Clockmakers from 1520* (Felix Hudson, Dunfermline, 1982), which contains biographical data on local clockmakers from the sixteenth century onward; *Old Stirling Clockmakers* (Charles Allan, Stirling, 1990), which includes a directory of clockmakers back to mid-sixteenth century; *Clock and Watchmakers of Central Scotland, 1537-1900* (Donald Whyte, Edinburgh); *Clock and*

*Watchmakers of the West of Scotland* (Donald Whyte, Edinburgh); *Clock and Watchmakers of the Scottish Highlands, 1780-1900* (Donald Whyte, Edinburgh); *Clock and Watchmakers of the Tay Valley, 1554-1900* (Donald Whyte, Edinburgh).

Sir James D. Marwick's *Edinburgh Guilds and Crafts* (Edinburgh,1899) is a sketch of the history of burgess-ship, guild brotherhood, and membership of crafts in the city. Another publication regarding Edinburgh guilds is *List of the Deans of Guild of the City of Edinburgh, from 1403 to 1890* (T. G. Stevenson, Edinburgh, 1890).

*Roll of Apprentices of Aberdeen, 1622-1796* (Frances J. McDonnell, Baltimore, 2015), has, for example, the following listings:

> Alexander Gellan, son of Alexander Gellan, a butcher
> in Aberdeen, was apprenticed to John Wallace a
> shoemaker, for five years from 12 April 1781. No fee.
> The father and John Henderson a wool-comber were
> cautioners (i.e. guarantors); John Kilgour, lawful son of
> the late Thomas Kilgour, sometime watchmaker in the
> burgh of Inverness, with the consent of William McLean,
> a goldsmith, the curator nominated by his father, was
> apprenticed to Andrew Jaffrey, a merchant, for five years
> from April 1711.

*Register of Edinburgh Apprentices, 1666-1700 and 1701-1755*, two volumes (C. B. Boog-Watson, Edinburgh, 1929), tells us that Hector Monro, son of Daniel Monro in Sutherland, was apprenticed to David Chrysty, a periwigmaker in Edinburgh on 28 August 1689, and William Sheriff, son of Alexander Sheriff, a janitor, was apprenticed to Hugh Barclay a clockmaker in Edinburgh on 6 December 1727; while the *Register of Edinburgh Apprentices, 1756-1800* (Marguerite Wood, Edinburgh, 1963) completes the published series. Some Scots living in the colonies sent their children to Scotland to serve an apprenticeship under Scottish craftsmen:

> Robert Stevenson, son of Allan Stevenson a storekeeper in
> St. Kitts, was apprenticed to Thomas Smith, a white-iron
> smith in Edinburgh, on 2 June 1796 for six years.

Some other publications regarding trades include *History of the Skinners, Furriers and Glovers of Glasgow* (Harry Lumsden, Glasgow, 1937), which has a list of members from 1516 to 1936; *Annals of the Skinners Craft in Glasgow, 1516 to 1616* (William Whyte, Glasgow, 1870); *Sketch of the Incorporation of Masons and the Lodge of Glasgow St. John* (James Cruikshank, Glasgow, 1879), which has individual biographies of builders in Glasgow in 1824, lists of benefactors from 1697, a roll of Deacon Convenor of the Trades of Glasgow from 1604 to 1879, etc.; *The Baxter Books of St. Andrews, from 1548 to 1861* (J. H. MacAdam, Leith, 1903), which is based on the minutes of the proceedings of the Incorporation of Bakers and has lists of officials and men admitted to the craft or trade; *The Incorporation of Bakers of Stirling* (David B. Morris, Stirling, 1923); and *The Incorporation of Bakers of Glasgow* (Glasgow, 1931).

*The Incorporation of Bonnet-makers and Dyers of Glasgow* (Glasgow, 1920) has lists of deacons from 1604 to 1919 and lists of members from 1866 to 1919, for example, "men such as Thomas F Hamilton, of 97 West George Street, Glasgow, who was admitted to the Dyer Craft in 1872." Also see *The Incorporation of Dyers and Bonnet-makers in Glasgow* (W. H. Hill, Glasgow, 1875); *The Young Dyers of Galashiels* (P. Sulley, Galashiels, 1919); *History of the Incorporation of Bonnet-makers and Dyers of Glasgow, 1597-1950* (Matthew Lindsay, Glasgow, 1952); *The Directory of Ladies of Pleasure in Edinburgh* (Edinburgh, 1745, reprinted in 1978 in Edinburgh); *The Ancient Lists of Office Bearers from 1738, Records of the Weaver Society of Anderston* (Glasgow, 1879); *The Records of the Incorporation of Tailors of Glasgow* (J. M. Taylor, Glasgow, 1872); *Maltmen, Customs and Excisemen of Dundee, 1700-1850* (Ada Pellow, Dundee, 1991); *Chronicles and History of the Maltman Craft or Incorporation of Glasgow, 1605-1895* (F. G. Dougall, Glasgow, 1895); *The Incorporation of Wrights in Glasgow* (J. M. Reid, Glasgow, 1928), which includes a list of members and their addresses from 1800 to 1928, for example, "James Gray, a wright of Hill Street, Gallowgate, Glasgow, who was admitted in 1839"; *Old Glasgow Weavers: The Incorporation of Weavers, 1514-1981* (Robert D. McEwan, Glasgow, 1981), which contains the names of the brethren of the craft on 5 May 1593, a list of deacons from 1591 to 1982, a list of clerks to the Incorporation from 1600 to 1968, a roll of members from 1795 to 1981, etc.; *Painters in Scotland, from 1301 to 1700, a Biographical Dictionary* (M. R. Apted and Susan Hannabuss, Edinburgh, 1978); "Renfrewshire Cart-wright Society, from 1799 to 1817" in the *Renfrewshire Family History Society Journal* # 40 (Gourock, 2019); *Dumfries Silversmiths* (K. H. Dobie, Dumfries, 1985), which has lists and biographical data from 1710 to 1896; *The Lanarkshire Miners, from 1775 to 1974* (A. B. Campbell, Edinburgh, 1979); and *The Scottish Miners* (R. Page Arnot, London, 1955).

*Edinburgh Goldsmiths' Minutes 1525 to 1700* (Fotheringham, Edinburgh, 2006) contains information such as the following:

> Act against prenteisses for disserting thir masters service
> and playing at cards and dyce, 10 Martii 1660') and
> ('V Januarij 1621, The whilk day compeirit Gilbert
> Kirkwood and with him Thomas Kirkwood sonne lauful
> to umquhile Adam Kirkwood indweller in Collingtoun
> and producit ane indentour of the dait the penult of
> December 1620 quhairin he is bund for the space of ten
> yeiris and ane year for meit and fie and hes payet fourtie
> schillingis.

**Records in Archives.** Records in the Glasgow City Archives include Glasgow Chimney Sweeps, from 1852 to 1862; Trades House of Glasgow, from 1597 to 1775 (GCA.T-TH1); Hammermen of Glasgow, from 1616 to 1934 (GCA.T-TH2); Tailors of Glasgow, from 1504 to 1974 (GCA.T-TH3); Cordiners of Glasgow, from 1550 to 1961 (GCA.T-TH4); Weavers of Glasgow, from 1504 to 1974 (GCA.T-TH5); Maltmen of Glasgow, from 1615 to 1977 (GCA.T-TH6); Bakers of Glasgow, from 1574 to 1961 (GCA.T-TH7); Skinners of Glasgow, from the Thirteenth Century to 1976 (GCA.T-TH8); Coopers of Glasgow, from the Thirteenth Century to 1976 (GCA.T-TH10); Fleshers of Glasgow, from 1576 to 1968 (GCA.T-TH11); Masons of Glasgow, from the Fourteenth Century to 1976 (GCA.T-TH12); Gardeners of Glasgow, from 1626 to 1956 (GCA.T-TH13); Barbers of Glasgow, from 1656 to 1962 (GCA.T-TH14); Bonnet-makers and Dyers of Glasgow, from the Thirteenth Century to 1957 (GCA.T-TH15); Framework Knitters and Stocking-makers of Glasgow, from 1756 to 1904 (GCA.T-TH16); Weavers of Anderston, from 1754 to 1985 (GCA.T-TH17 and TD1615); Hammermen of Calton, from 1789 to 1854 (GCA.TD105); Weavers of Govan, from 1756 from 1963 (GCA.TD1740); Weavers of Rutherglen, from 1641 to 1871 (GCA.RU9.1); Journeymen Bakers' Society of Glasgow, Roll of Members, from 1765 to 1799 (GCA.TD200.14); The Wrights of Glasgow, from 1650 to 1977 (GCA.T-TH9).

Edinburgh City Archives has the following records pertaining to the various trades and crafts located in and around Edinburgh: Incorporation of the Tailors of Leith, from 1730 to 1824 (ECA.SL.229); Incorporation of Traffickers of Leith, from 1744 to 1816 (ECA.SL228); Incorporation of Wrights and Masons of Edinburgh, from 1669 to 1910, which includes the register of apprentices (ECA.SL34); Incorporation of the Trades of the Canongate from 1561 to 1856 (ECA.SL151); Incorporation of Bakers in Edinburgh from 1522 to 1958 (ECA.SL33); Incorporation of the Carters of Leith, from 1556 to 1823 (ECA.SL226); Incorporation of Coopers of Leith, from 1550 to 1873 (ECA.SL220); Incorporation of the Hammermen of Edinburgh, from 1494 to 2000 (ECA.ED8); Incorporation of the Hammermen of Leith, from 1730 to 1800 (ECA.SL.230); Incorporation of the Hammermen of the Canongate, from 1610 to 1861 (ECA.SL69); Incorporation of the Porters of Leith, from 1770 to 1879 (ECA.SL231); Incorporation of the Journeymen Coopers of Leith, from 1806 to 1837 (ECA.SL68); Edinburgh Street Porters Records from 1762 to 1849 (ECA.SL235); Incorporation of the Skinners and Furriers of Edinburgh, from 1603 to 1903 (ECA.Accn.617); Leith Association of Metters and Weighers, from 1704 to 1989 (ECA.SL85).

The National Register of Archives' records include Incorporation of Hammermen in Haddington (NRAS.202/2); Incorporation of Hammermen in Dumbarton from 1799 to 1829 (NRAS.547.5.3); Incorporation of Smiths in Kirkcaldy from 1801 to 1832 (NRAS.744/16); Incorporation of Wrights in Perth, from 1538 (NRAS.1128). Incorporation of Fleshers in Perth from 1634 to 1967 (NRAS.1994); Incorporation of Fleshers of Galashiels, in 1706 (NRAS.3894); Bakers Incorporation of Perth (NRAS.1071.14.3); Incorporation of Bakers in Aberdeen (NRAS.729); Incorporation of Tailors in Aberdeen from 1593 (NRAS.730); Tailors of Linktown of Abbotshall (NRAS.744/13); Glover Incorporation of Perth, from 1329 to 1886 (NRAS.368); Stationers of Glasgow from 1740 to

1923 (NRAS.396/175); Incorporation of Shoemakers of Banff from 1655 to 1825 (NRAS.2599); Incorporation of Trades of Kirkwall, from 1767 to 1968 (NRAS.2933); Incorporation of Weavers in Perth, 1593 to 1975 (NRAS.1227).

Dundee City Archives has Records of the Hammerman Incorporation of Dundee from 1587 to 2014, which includes a Register of Journeymen from 1658 to 1795 (DCA.GD.HF.H.1; also NRAS.1181/1); Records of the Incorporation of Maltmen of Dundee, from 1653, including Registers of Apprentices, 1653 to 1847 (DCA.GD.HF.M.2/1); Lists of Pensioners from 1692 (DCA.GD.HF.M.5/1).

Stirling Archives has a substantial collection of records of local trades, including Incorporation of Trades from 1574 to 1966; Incorporation of Bakers from 1797 to 1962; Incorporation of Cordiners from 1655 to 1854; Incorporation of Fleshers from 1658 to 1914; Incorporation of Hammermen from 1596 to 1916; Incorporation of Maltmen from 1603 to 1911; Incorporation of Mechanics from 1636 to 1883; Incorporation of Skinners from 1579 to 1898; Incorporation of Tailors from 1556 to 1869; and the Incorporation of Weavers from 1600 to 1983.

The National Library of Scotland has records of the Incorporation of Tailors of the Canongate from 1438 to 1796 (NLS.1958).

## MISCELLANEOUS URBAN RECORDS

***Publications.*** *A Directory of Edinburgh in 1752* (James Gilhooley, Edinburgh, 1988) is an excellent source that lists inhabitants by name, occupation, and address; it also includes a trade directory listing people by occupations. *Edinburgh House-Mails Taxation Book, 1634-1636* (A. Allen and C. Spence, SHS, Edinburgh, 2014), based on a manuscript in Edinburgh City Archives (ECA.HTB*)*, is another excellent source, listing all landlords with their occupations, all the houses of Edinburgh, taxes due, and all tenants and their occupations. *The Examination Roll of Arbroath of 1751 and the Town's Duty Roll of 1753* (Flora Davidson, SRS, Edinburgh, 1987) lists all inhabitants of the burgh, with their addresses, occupation, and religious denomination. See also *The Royal Company of*

*Archers, 1675-1951* (Ian Hay, Edinburgh, 1951) and Michael Lynch's *The Early Modern Town in Scotland* (Wolfboro, 1987).

Scots abroad wishing to progress in society or business had to prove their credentials before being accepted as a citizen or burgess. They would write home for a birth brief, as described in *Birth Briefs of Aberdeen, 1637-1705* (F. J. McDonnell, St. Andrews, 1995):

> Robert Lovell, son of John Lovell of Brunsie and his
> wife Margaret Murdoch, wishing to become a burgess of
> Radaune in Poland, obtained a birth brief from Dundee
> Town Council on 10 February 1611.

***Records in Archives.*** The NRS has Glasgow Street Directories from 1783-1978 (in GCA); Lists of Inhabitants of Perth in 1773 (NRS.B59.24.1.40); Lists of Inhabitants of Perth in 1766 (NRS.B59.24.1.36); and Indentures of the Apprentices of Perth, 1748-1784 (NRS.B59.79.172).

Dundee City Archives has Dundee Directories from 1782. These, initially, listed the merchants and tradesmen with street addresses, also the Masonic Lodges with named officials and the magistrates; later directories were more wide-ranging.

## RURAL RECORDS

The records of landed families contain considerable information on their estates, tenants, workers, and others. Many of these records remain in private hands (see the National Register of Archives in Scotland), some are held in local archives and libraries, and a few have been published.

***Publications.*** *Survey of Loch Tayside in 1769* (Margaret McArthur, Edinburgh, 1936) is based on documents made by two surveyors, John Farquharson and John McArthur. It identifies every farm or habitation on the sides of Loch Tay, names the tenants, and describes the quality of the land and the crops; for example, it tells us that at Wester Carawhin the inhabitants were Duncan McIllihuas, John McAll, John McDiarmid, Finlay McGrigor, Donald McDiarmid, John McInlaroy, Finlay McDiarmid, William McVourich, and John Malloch.

*The Inhabitants of the Argyll Estate in 1779* (Eric R. Cregeen, Edinburgh, 1963) is an excellent source for those with ancestry in Argyll, as it is a virtual census and record of the names, ages, status, occupations, and families of the tacksmen, tenants, sub-tenants, cottars, farm-servants, domestics, inn-keepers, ferrymen, and others on the lands of the Duke of Argyll in Argyll. For example, it tells us that on the farm of Kenchregan were Donald McLean, a herd, aged 42; his wife, Ann McIntyre, aged 36; his daughter Peggy Sinclair, aged 12; his son John Sinclair, aged 10; his son Patrick Sinclair, aged 6; his son Gilbert Sinclair, aged 4; his daughter Catherine Sinclair, aged 1; and his servant Margaret McIntyre, aged 20. *Argyll Estate Instructions, Mull, Morvern, Tiree, 1771-1805* (Eric R. Creegan, Edinburgh, 1964) provides insight into how the Duke of Argyll and his chamberlains operated and developed the estate, and gives the names of tenants and farms.

*The Calendar of Writs of Munro of Foulis from 1299 to 1823* (C. T. Innes, Edinburgh, 1940) is a collection of legal documents dealing with the family's property in the north of Scotland, for example:

> Writ 279, dated 8 September 1688. Disposition by
> Alexander Monro of Catwell to George Dallas of St.
> Martins, land in the barony of Foulis, parish of Kiltearn.

*The Binns Papers, 1320 to 1864* (Sir James Dalyell, Edinburgh, 1938) deals with the estate and family of Dalyell of Binns through its documents:

> Number 535 a discharge by James Stephen, schoolmaster
> at Carriden, for a year's salary payable from the lands of
> Binns. Dated at Carriden 12 April 1721.

*A Directory of Landownership in Scotland, around 1770* (L. R. Timperley, Edinburgh, 1976) identifies the landowners and their lands, organized by counties; *The Commons of Argyll* (Duncan C. Mactavish, Lochgilphead, 1935) lists inhabitants and their places of residence in 1685 and 1692.

**Records in Archives.** Perth and Kinross Archives has the records of the Threipland Estates in Perthshire and in Caithness, which identify members of the family, friends, relatives, tenants, and workers there—

for example, "Robert Innes, a servant to William Sinclair of Dunbeath, Caithness, a witness on 10 April 1590" (PKA.169.1.3.1) and "William McBetytre in Stirling on 11 June 1631" (PKA.169.1.2.10).

Highland Archives in Inverness has the Baillie of Dunain estate papers from 1705 and the Munro of Navar estate papers from 1670, among others. Included in the estate papers held in Stirling Archives are those from 1494 to 1912 of Drummond of Blair-Drummond.

The Borthwick family of Crookston estate papers from 1656 to 1986 are partly in the National Records of Scotland (NRS.GD350) and partly in the National Library of Scotland, from 1779 to 1868 (NLS.Acc.13699). Shetland Archives has the Bruce of Symbister papers from the sixteenth to the twentieth century (ZA.GD144), as well as the Morton Estate papers (ZA.GD150).

## PROFESSIONS

Below are some publications about various common professions.

**Accountants.** *A History of the Chartered Accountants of Scotland from the Earliest Times to 1954* (Edinburgh, 1954).

**Actuaries.** *The History of the Faculty of Actuaries in Scotland, 1856-1956* (A. Davidson, Edinburgh, 1956).

**Architects.** *Architects and Architecture in Dundee, 1770-1914* (D. M. Walker, Dundee, 1977).

**Banks.** Banking companies in Scotland date from the late seventeenth century. Before that, many banking functions were done by goldsmiths. There are several published histories of the main Scottish banks, whose number has diminished over the years due to mergers: *History of the Royal Bank of Scotland, 1727-1927* (Neil Munro, Edinburgh, 1928); *Our Bank: The Commercial Bank of Scotland, 1810-1946* (Edinburgh, 1946); *Scottish Banking, 1695-1973* (S. G. Checkland, Glasgow, 1975); *The Bank of Scotland, 1695-1945* (Charles A. Malcolm, Edinburgh, 1945); *The British Linen Bank, 1746-1946* (Charles A. Malcolm, Edinburgh,

1950); *A History of the Union Bank of Scotland* (Robert S. Rait, Glasgow, 1930); *The National Bank of Scotland Centenary, 1825-1925* (Edinburgh, 1925); *The Royal Bank of Scotland, 1727-1977* (Edinburgh, 1977); and *The Scottish Provincial Banking Companies, 1747-1864* (Charles W. Munn, Edinburgh, 1981).

**Lawyers, Solicitors, or Writers.** There are two types of lawyers in Scotland—there are advocates who work in the Court of Session, the supreme civil court, and there are solicitors, alias writers, who work in the Sheriff Courts and fulfill other legal duties. Publications include *A History of the Society of Writers to H. M. Signet, with lists of members from 1594 to 1890* (Edinburgh, 1890); *The Register of the Society of Writers to H. M. Signet* (Edinburgh, 1983); *History of the Writers to H.M. Signet* (Edinburgh, 1936), which contains a list of members from 1594 to 1935; *Index Judicus: The Scottish Law List 1846-1961* (Edinburgh, 1962); *The Faculty of Advocates in Scotland, 1532-1943, with genealogical notes* (Edinburgh 1944), which contains an alphabetical list of Advocates, with information such as the following:

> Henry Baxter of Idvies, son of John Baxter of Idvies, a
> banker in Dundee, was admitted to the Faculty of Advocates
> on 10 June 1828, married Elizabeth Dorothy Laing, only
> daughter of Samuel Laing of Papdale, died on 16 August
> 1837.

*A History of the Society of Advocates in Aberdeen* (Aberdeen, 1912) includes information about members from 1549 to 1911, for example:

> Thomas Primrose, born 11 December 1808, son of
> Reverend William Primrose, a minister in Aberdeen, and
> his wife Isabella Gibb, educated at Aberdeen Grammar
> School, graduated MA from Marischal College, Aberdeen,
> apprenticed to Charles Chalmers an Advocate in Aberdeen,
> was admitted to the Society of Advocates in Aberdeen on 10
> June 1833, went to the United States to wind up the affairs
> of the North American Investment and Insurance Company,
> subsequently practised in America, died, unmarried, in
> Aberdeen on 18 January 1886.

*The Court of the Lord Lyon, 1318-1945* (Sir Francis James Grant, Edinburgh, 1945) identifies the officers since the medieval period of the Lyon Court, which basically supervises heraldry in Scotland. For example:

> Sir William Stewart of Luthrie, Ross Herald from 1565
> to 20 February 1567 when he became Lord Lyon, he was
> deprived of his office in 1568 as fugitive in a conspiracy
> for the Regent's slaughter by sorcery and necromancy,
> burnt at St. Andrews for witchcraft in August 1569.

There are also records of notaries in the NRS from 1563, but they are only continuous beginning in 1661. The Register of Notaries can provide useful information, such as "on 17 June 1742, Andrew Shand, a writer in Thurso, son of Andrew Shand, tenant at Innes in the parish of Urquhart, was admitted as a notary public" (NRS.NP.2.24). Publications include *The Admission Register of Notaries Public in Scotland, from 1800 to 1899* (J. Finlay, Edinburgh, 2018) and *The Old Minute Book of the Faculty of Procurators in Glasgow, 1668-1758* (J. S. Muirhead, Glasgow, 1948).

**Ministers.** *Fasti Ecclesiae Scoticanae*, 10 volumes (H. Scott, Edinburgh, 1920s-1981) gives biographical data on every parish minister of the Church of Scotland since 1560. Other publications include *Biographical Sketches of Early Scottish Congregational Ministers, 1798-1851* (R. Kinniburgh, Edinburgh, 1851) and *The Catholic Hierarchy of Scotland* (J. S. Burns, 1986)

**Physicians, Doctors, and Surgeons.** Many of the early medical practitioners served apprenticeships under qualified men. Later, a university education was essential. Sometimes a qualified and well-experienced man would apply for recognition from a university, so the registers of apprentices as well as the university graduation rolls should be checked. The universities of Leiden and of Edinburgh were the leading schools of medicine in the eighteenth century.

Publications include *History of Scottish Medicine to 1860*, second edition (J. D. Comrie, Edinburgh, 1930); *Memorials of the Faculty of Physicians and Surgeons of Glasgow from 1599 to 1850* (A. Duncan, Glasgow, 1896); *Physicians, Surgeons, and Apothecaries. Medicine in Seventeenth Century Edinburgh* (Helen M. Dingwall, East Linton, 1995); and *Sketch of the*

*History of the Faculty of Physicians and Surgeons of Glasgow* (W. Weir, Glasgow, 1868).

*History of the Royal College of Physicians of Edinburgh* (W. S. Craig, Oxford, 1976) lists members from 1696 to 1975 and office bearers from 1681 to 1975. *Royal College of Surgeons of Edinburgh* (Edinburgh, 1874) lists fellows from 1581 to 1873.

**Stockbrokers.** Publications include *Records of the Glasgow Stock Association, 1844-1898* (Maclehose, Glasgow, 1898) and *Records of the Glasgow Stock Association, 1844-1926* (Jackson Wylie, Glasgow, 1927).

## THE COVENANTERS

The Covenanters date from 1638, when members of the Church of Scotland who were opposed to the attempts of King Charles I to impose an Episcopal structure on the Church and bring it in line with the Church of England subscribed to a document known as the National Covenant. The Covenant pledged the signatories to mutual defense and prepared for a military reaction by King Charles, who was raising an army in England with the aim of invading Scotland, though he had problems raising the money to finance it. The Scots invaded northern England, defeated the English at Newburn, and then occupied Newcastle. Charles sued for peace, which was agreed upon in 1641. In 1662 the government of King Charles II restored episcopacy on the largely Presbyterian Scots, which led to conventicles, persecution, and a Covenanter Rising in 1666. This was repeated in 1679 during the reign of King James VII and II, whom the militants suspected was aiming to return the church to Catholicism. The Covenanters were defeated by the king's forces at the Battle of Bothwell Brig in 1679, and then the "killing time" occurred, which caused many Presbyterians to take refuge in Ireland, Holland, and America.

During the 1680s the government in Edinburgh—faced with a virtual rebellion, mainly in the South of Scotland, by militant Protestant Covenanters—attempted to identify the Covenanters by listing the inhabitants of parishes. These parish lists are recorded in the published *Register of the Privy Council of Scotland*, Volume IX. For example, in October

1684, there is "A list of the names of the disorderly persons in the parish of Dalton. Helen Grierson, William Kennedy, Janet Aitcheson, Agnes Johnstone, Nicolas Johnstone, Robert Nicolson, William Carruthers, Christopher Carruthers, George Wallace and Margaret Gibson his wife and daughter, Robert Armstrong, Anna Armstrong, John Bell, and David Gass," thereafter is a complete list of every person within the parish of Dalton, above twelve years of age. These lists identify hundreds of residents by parish and farm throughout the counties of the South West. Sometimes the records note that specified individuals had fled to Ireland or to Holland.

**Publications**. *A Regimental History of the Covenanting Armies, 1639-1651* (Edward M. Furgol, Edinburgh, 1990); *Parish Lists of Wigtownshire and Minnigaff, 1684* (William Scott, Edinburgh 1916), which identifies 9,276 residents of Wigtownshire in 1684 and is based on the government records used to identify the Covenanter "rebels"; *Men of the Covenant* (A. Smellie, Glasgow, 1911); *The Covenanters* (J. K. Hewison, 1908); *The Covenanters of Ayrshire* (R. Lawson, Paisley, 1887); *The Covenanters of the Merse* (J. W. Brown, Edinburgh, 1893); *The Scottish Covenanters* (James Barr, 1947); and *The Scottish Covenanters, from 1660 to 1688* (Ian B. Cowan, London, 1976).

# MILITARY RECORDS

The British Army and Royal Navy personnel records are at the following locations:

- The National Archives Kew, Richmond, Surrey, TW9 4DU; www.nationalarchives.gov.uk/

- National Army Museum; Royal Hospital Road, Chelsea, SW3 4HT; www.nam.ac.uk/

- National Maritime Museum, Greenwich, London SE10 9NF; www.rmg.co.uk/national-maritime-museum

- RAF Museum, Grahame Park Way, London, NW9 5LL; www.rafmuseum.org.uk/london/ (has Army lists for officers from the 1740s; Navy lists for officers from 1782)

The Royal Air Force was formed in 1918—the National Archives has personnel records for AIR1 and AIR79.

**Publications**. *Papers Relating to the Army of the Solemn League and Covenant*, two volumes (Edinburgh, 1917); *Miscellany of the Scottish History Society: Dundee Court Martial Records 1651* (during the occupation of Dundee by the Parliamentary Army); *The Scots Army, 1661-1688* (Charles Dalton, London, 1909); *History of the Royal Scots Fusiliers, 1678-1918* (John Buchan, London, 1925); *Historical Record of the Royal Scots Fusiliers* (James Clarke, 1885); *History of the 2nd Dragoons, Royal Scots Greys* (Edward Almack, London, 1908); *A Regimental History of the Covenanting Armies* (E. A. Furgol, Edinburgh, 1990); *The Scots Army, 1661-1688, with Memoirs of the Commanders-in-chief* (Charles Dalton, London, 1909); *Pontius Pilate's Bodyguard: A History of the First or the Royal Regiment of Foot, The Royal Scots*, three volumes (R. H. Paterson, Edinburgh, 2000-2007); *The Scottish Regiments, 1633-1996* (P. Mileham, Staplehurst, 1996); *The Scottish Regiments, 1633-1987* (P. J. R. Mileham, New York, 1988); *The Society of Trained Bands of Edinburgh, 1663-1874* (William Skinner, Edinburgh, 1889).

## Highland Regiments

**Publications**. *The Inverness-shire Highlanders (97th Regiment of Foot) 1794-1796* (H. B. Mackintosh, Elgin, 1926); *The Gordon Highlanders, 2nd Battalion, as quartered at Banff, 1811-1812* (J. M. Bulloch, Aberdeen, 1916); *Historical Records of the 71st Regiment (Highland Light Infantry), 1777-1852* (Richard Cannon, 1852); *The 93rd Highlanders, 1799-1927* (A. E. J. Cavendish, Frome, 1928); *The Story of the Highland Regiments, 1725-1925* (Frederick Watson, London, 1925); *The History of the 91st Argyllshire Highlanders* (R. P. Dunn-Pattison, Edinburgh, 1910); *The History of the 51st (Highland) Division* (F. W. Brasher, Edinburgh, 1921); *The History of the Gordon Highlanders, 1794-1898* (C. Greenhill Gardyne, London, 1929); *History of the 91st (Princess Louise's) Argyll Highlanders, 1st Battalion, 1794-1894* (P. Groves, Edinburgh, 1894); *Historical*

*Records of the 79th Regiment of Foot (Cameron Highlanders)* (Robert Jamieson, Edinburgh, 1863); *Historical Records of the Queen's Own Cameron Highlanders*, two volumes (Edinburgh, 1909); *Officers of the Black Watch, 1725-1937* (Neil McMicking, Perth, 1937); *History of the 42nd Royal Highlanders (The Black Watch), 1729-1893* (Percy Groves, Edinburgh, 1893); *The 93rd Highlanders, Now the 2nd Battalion of the Argyll and Sutherland Highlanders, 1799-1927* (A. Cavendish, Frome, 1928); *Historical Records of the 93rd Sutherland Highlanders, 1800-1890* (James McVeigh, Dumfries, 1890); *The Black Watch: The History of the Royal Highland Regiment* (E. and A. Linklater, London, 1977); *History of the 42nd Royal Highlanders—the Black Watch, 1729-1893* (Percy Groves, Edinburgh, 1893); *Proud Heritage: The Story of the Highland Light Infantry*, four volumes (L. B. Oates, London, 1952-1963); *The Story of the Atholl Highlanders* (J. L. M. Stewart, Blair Atholl, 2000); *The Atholl Highlanders* (I. Moncreiffe, Derby); *Highland Furies: The Black Watch, 1739-1899* (V. Schofield, London, 2012); *Wellington's Highland Warriors, 1743-1815* (Stuart Reid, Barnsley, 2010); *Proud Heritage; The Story of the Highland Light Infantry*, four volumes (L. B. Oatts, London, 1952-1963); *Seaforth Highlanders* (J Sym, Aldershot, 1962); *The Raising of the 79th Highlanders* (L. MacLean, 1980); *Records of the 90th Regiment (Perthshire Light Infantry), listing officers 1795-1880* (A Delavoye, London, 1880); *Official Records of the Mutiny in the Black Watch in 1743* (H. D. McWilliams, London, 1910); *Highlander* (Stuart Reid, London, 2000); *The Seaforth Highlanders in South Africa, 1899-1902* (Edinburgh, 1904); *Seaforth Highlanders, 1793-1925* (Edinburgh, 1926).

*A Military History of Perthshire, 1660-1902* (Marchioness of Tullibardine, Perth, 1908) contains a roll of Perthshire soldiers in various regiments, especially the Black Watch, in the Boer War; photographs of officers; NCOs; and men, ranks, names, regiments, and origins.

| Name | Age | Height | Birthplace | Trade | Date | And Place of Enlistment |
|---|---|---|---|---|---|---|
| M'Pherson, Dougald | 19 | 5 ft. 4 in. | Ardnamurchan, Argyle | Miner | Jan. 13, 1776 | Fort William |
| M'Pherson, Duncan | 24 | 5 ft. 5½ in. | Ardclach, Nairn | Labourer | Jan. 16, 1776 | Fochabers |
| M'Pherson, Evan | 17 | 5 ft. 4 in. | Alvey, Inverness | Tailor | Dec. 29, 1775 | " |
| M'Queen, Alexander | 15 | 5 ft. 4 in. | Moye, Inverness | Shoemaker | Jan. 23, 1776 | " |
| Mat, William | 23 | 5 ft. 6½ in. | Auch, Inverness | Labourer | Jan. 20, 1776 | " |
| Melville, Alexander | 16 | 5 ft. 4 in. | Boharm, Banff | Labourer | Dec. 13, 1775 | Huntly |
| Morrison, James | 17 | 5 ft. 4 in. | Deskford, Banff | Heckler | Dec. 13, 1775 | Fochabers |
| Munro, Robert | 17 | 5 ft. 6 in. | Ardersier, Inverness | Chapman | Dec. 19, 1775 | " |
| Munster, William | 18 | 5 ft. 4½ in. | St. Andrews, Moray | Merchant | Dec. 21, 1775 | Elgin |
| Munster, Thomas | 19 | 5 ft. 6½ in. | Boyndie, Banff | Labourer | Jan. 8, 1776 | Fochabers |
| Munro, Charles | 17 | 5 ft. 3 in. | Knockando, Moray | Weaver | Dec. 9, 1775 | Huntly |
| Munro, Alexander | 23 | 5 ft. 6½ in. | Bellie, Banff | Labourer | Feb. 12, 1776 | Banff |
| Robertson, John | 25 | 5 ft. 6 in. | Deskford, Banff | " | Jan. 30, 1776 | Fochabers |
| Ross, Hugh | 20 | 5 ft. 2½ in. | Kincairn, Ross | " | Jan. 24, 1776 | " |
| Ross, John | 18 | 5 ft. 6 in. | Tarbart, Ross | " | Jan. 8, 1776 | " |
| Ross, James | 18 | 5 ft. 5 in. | Auldearn, Nairn | Merchant | Feb. 21, 1776 | Elgin |
| Simpson, Edward | 18 | 5 ft. 7 in. | Long Setton, Lincoln | Brickmaker | Jan. 10, 1776 | Fochabers |
| Sinclair, Charles | 17 | 5 ft. 4½ in. | Latheron, Caithness | Labourer | Jan. 8, 1776 | " |
| Sinclair, Francis | 18 | 5 ft. 5 in. | Latheron, Caithness | " | Feb. 14, 1776 | Banff |
| Smith, Peter | 18 | 5 ft. 5½ in. | Inverallan, Inverness | " | Jan. 8, 1776 | Fochabers |
| Smith, Robert | 16 | 5 ft. 4 in. | Cairnie, Aberdeen | " | Jan. 8, 1776 | " |
| Stalker, James | 15 | 5 ft. 3 in. | Raffart, Moray | " | Dec. 18, 1775 | " |
| Stephen, William | 16 | 5 ft. 5 in. | Elgin, Elgin | " | Dec. 26, 1776 | Elgin |
| Stewart, Allan | 19 | 5 ft. 4½ in. | Cromdale, Moray | " | Jan. 1, 1776 | Fochabers |
| Stewart, James | 18 | 5 ft. 5 in. | Kirkmichael, Banff | " | Jan. 6, 1776 | " |
| Sutherland, James | 19 | 5 ft. 4½ in. | Elgin, Moray | " | Dec. 13, 1775 | Elgin |
| Sutherland, Neill | 16 | 5 ft. 5 in. | Latheron, Caithness | " | Dec. 15, 1775 | Fochabers |
| Syme, Alexander | 20 | 5 ft. 4 in. | Grange, Banff | " | Dec. 29, 1775 | " |
| Taylor, James | 18 | 5 ft. 3½ in. | Elgin, Moray | " | Dec. 25, 1775 | Elgin |
| Thomas, Alexander | 18 | 5 ft. 4 in. | Fochabers, Moray | " | Dec. 30, 1775 | Fochabers |
| Thomas, James | 16 | 5 ft. 5 in. | Fochabers, Moray | " | Dec. 20, 1775 | " |
| Thomson, Peter, Sergt. | 35 | 5 ft. 6½ in. | Dyke, Moray | " | Dec. 7, 1775 | " |
| Petrie, James | 17 | 5 ft. 4 in. | Dundurcas, Moray | Labourer | Dec. 29, 1775 | Huntly |
| Tulloch, David | 25 | 5 ft. 6 in. | Ardclach, Nairn | Squarewright | Dec. 14, 1775 | Gordon Castle |
| Tulloch, John | 20 | 5 ft. 6½ in. | Ardclach, Nairn | Labourer | Jan. 18, 1776 | Fochabers |
| Tulloch, Robert | 20 | 5 ft. 4 in. | Nairn, Nairn | " | Dec. 5, 1775 | " |
| Watson, Donald | 18 | 5 ft. 4½ in. | Rosemarky, Ross | Daylabourer | Dec. 5, 1775 | " |
| Watt, John | 40 | 5 ft. 5 in. | Kennethmont, Aberdeen | Labourer | Feb. 6, 1776 | Huntly |

The 71st was reduced in 1783, and Captain Maxwell afterwards entered the 74th Regiment. It is a curious fact that the 71st now forms the first battalion of the Highland Light Infantry, while the 74th is the second battalion. It may have been Maxwell's connection with the 74th that led his brother-in-law, the 4th Duke of Gordon, to enlist six men for Captain Twysden's company of the 74th in 1787, as follows:—

| | | Age | Height | Bounty |
|---|---|---|---|---|
| Nov. 4—John Duncan, hosier, | Speymouth | 16 | 5 ft. 4 in. | £5 5 0 |
| " 19—William Mitchell | | 24 | 5 ft. 9 in. | 5 5 0 |
| " 20—Hugh Gordon | | 29 | 5 ft. 6 in. | 3 8 0 |
| " 20—John Bonniman | | 30 | 5 ft. 5½ in. | 3 8 0 |
| " 27—Hugh Ellis | | 17 | 5 ft. 4½ in. | 5 5 0 |
| Dec. 3—Sergeant Alexander Sutherland; not attested, but supposed absent | | 30 | 5 ft. 11 in. | |

† Deserted.
‡ The Duchess sent his wife a boll of meal.
§ Discharged—having an ulcer on his thigh.

List of the 71st regiment, known as Fraser's Highlanders *(courtesy of the Spalding Club)*

## Lowland Regiments

**Publications.** *The Lowland Scots Regiments, Their Origin, Character and Services Previous to the Great War of 1914* (Herbert Maxwell, Glasgow, 1918); *History of the Royal Scots* (T. B. Simon, Edinburgh, 1943); *A History of the 3rd Battalion, King's Own Scottish Borderers, 1798-1907* (R. W. Weir, Dumfries, 1907); *A Short History of the Cameronians (Scottish*

*Rifles)* (H. C. Wylly, Aldershot, 1925); *The Cameronians (Scottish Rifles): The Story of a Regiment* (Douglas Ferrier, Glasgow, 1919); *History of the Cameronians (Scottish Rifles)*, four volumes (S. H. F. Johnston, H. H. Johnston, C. N. Barclay, J. Baynes, Aldershot, 1957-1971); "The Scots Brigade in the Eighteenth Century" (S. Conway, in *Northern Scotland*, volume one, 2010); *The History of the Scots Guards*, two volumes (F. Maurice, London, 1934); *History of the Ayrshire Yeomanry Cavalry* (W. S. Cooper, Edinburgh, 1881); *A History of the Fife Light Horse* (A. Thomson, Edinburgh, 1892); *Queen's Own Royal Glasgow Yeomanry, 1848-1948* (Glasgow, 1948); *All The Blue Bonnets: The History of the King's Own Scottish Borderers* (R. Woolcombe, London, 1980); *The History of the Scots Guards* (F. Maurice, London, 1934); *The Fife and Forfar Yeomanry, 1914-1919* (D. Ogilvie, London, 1921); *Muster Roll of Angus; South African War, 1899-1900* (J. B. Salmond, Arbroath, 1900)—an excellent source as it identifies 170 men, names, addresses, occupations, with photos of every man in uniform!

## Militia

During the medieval era the feudal system required lords, barons, and others who held land of the Crown to supply soldiers for the king when required. These were the militias or fencibles of the period, which supplemented any standing army of the king. Some of these local militias were the forerunners of many of the Highland regiments raised during the eighteenth century, for example the Gordon Highlanders. The Heritable Jurisdiction Act of 1747 broke the feudal power of the landowners, and made them unable to raise troops, as they had in 1715 and 1745. The burghs also had their own militias, which were to defend the burghs as well as support the king's army when required. In 1778, and later in 1793, due to the perceived threat from America and France, the British Government authorized the raising of fencibles, volunteers trained in military skills.

***Records in Archives***. Aberdeen City Archives has the muster rolls of the Aberdeenshire Militia for 1803 and 1804. It also has lists of appeals to the Aberdeen Commissioners concerning impressment 1757-1758 to raise troops for the Seven Years War, including the French and Indian

War. These lists provide the names of the militiamen and their place of residence. There is also a collection of certificates granted for the relief of the wives and children of the militiamen between 1803 and 1816 (ACA. AS.Mil.6-1/6). Aberdeen City Archives also has the muster roll of the Fraserburgh Volunteers of 1803 (AS.Amil.8.9.1-3).

Dundee Militia Lists of 1801 identify hundreds of men between sixteen and forty years old, with their occupations and addresses, who were eligible to serve in the local militia to oppose an anticipated French invasion during the Napoleonic Wars (NRS.SC47.72.3). Glasgow City Archives has a similar list for Glasgow, but covering the period 1810-1831, as well as lists for Angus, Lanarkshire, Renfrewshire, Argyll, Stirling, Caithness, and Perthshire, giving name of soldier, parish, wife, and children (GCA.D-TC12).

Edinburgh City Archives has Army attestation papers from 1794 to 1887 (ECA.SL54); militia records from 1717 to 1894 (ECA. SL.127), notably consisting of lists of persons eligible to serve; and records of volunteer regiments from 1846 to 1892 (ECA.SL126), which include returns of enrolled men and officers.

Perth and Kinross Archives hold local militia papers dating between 1680 and 1891, with the emphasis being on the period 1785 to 1820 (PKA.PE66). The papers include petitions by men illegally enlisted. For example, William Steele, a weaver in Bridgend, Perth, claimed that he was illegally enlisted into the Scots Brigade by Lieutenant James McBean, on 26 March 1803 (PKA.PE66/1); Kenneth McLeod, a weaver in Perth, claimed that he was illegally enlisted into the 7th Regiment of Foot by Corporal Robert Roy, and was discharged on 12 November 1810 (PKA.66/1). Other records include items such as receipts for money paid to the families in Dunkeld of militiamen in 1799, including Margaret Jones, wife of Peter Murray with three children; C. Inches, the wife of Alexander McKenzie; and the wives of Joseph Robertson and John Clarke (PKA.66.77).

Dumfries and Galloway Archives has the Dumfries Militia records from 1744 to 1804 (DGA.ED9); the Dumfries Militia recruitment book from

1744 to 1779 (DGA.ED9.1.1); Dumfries Militia pay lists from 1798 to 1799 (DGA.EGD27.1-6); Dumfries Militia muster lists from 1804 to 1811 (DGA.EGD27.4.2-4); Dumfries Volunteers muster book from 1860 to 1914 (DGA.WIWMS.2009.30.30); and the Kirkcudbrightshire Militia, wives and families from 1802 to 1816 (DGA.EK9.2.1-8).

The National Records of Scotland has the papers of the Royal Linlithgow Militia and Yeomanry, 1668 to 1810 (NRS.B48.16.8.1) and the Registers of the East Lothian Militia, 1680-1683 (NRS.PC15/15). The Fife Archives has Kinross Militia, 1716, which gives details of payments to men (FA.A/AAF/40.30.4.1) and Commissions of Deputy Lieutenants and Militia Officers from 1841 to 1869 (FA.FCC.22.1.3).

*Publications.* "An Angus Militia List of the 1670s," in *The Historian* (Dundee, October 2019; based on NRS.GD16.53.39); *The Great Scottish Volunteer Review of 1860* (E. R. Vernon, Edinburgh, 1860), listing thousands of men with ranks, units, or regiments; *A History of the Kinross-shire Volunteers* (N. H. Walker, Kinross, 1988); *Galston Parish, Militia 1788-1801* (Troon, 2003); *Records of the Scottish Volunteer Force, 1859-1900* (J. M. Grierson, Edinburgh, 1909); *A History of the Volunteers of Clackmannan and Kinross* (E. Dyer, Alva, 1907), mainly covering the Boer War; *The Elgin Fencibles, 1794-1892* (D. McNaughton, Dunfermline, 1994); *List of Fencible Men in the Earl of Airlie's Lands, 1643* (J. Blair, Dundee, 2001); *The Kincardineshire Volunteers from 1798 to 1816* (William Will, Aberdeen, 1920); *History of the 7th Lanarkshire Rifle Volunteers* (James Orr, 1884); *Records of the Ayrshire Militia from 1802 to 1883* (Edinburgh, 1884); *A History of the Aberdeen Volunteers* (Donald Sinclair, Aberdeen, 1907); *The Reay Fencibles, (Lord Reay's Highlanders)* (John Mackay, Glasgow, 1890); *The Grant, Strathspey or 1st Highland Fencible Regiment, 1793-1799* (H. B. Mackintosh, Elgin, 1934); *The Northern or Gordon Fencibles, 1778-1783* (H. B. Mackintosh, Edinburgh, 1929); *History of the Reay Fencible Highland Regiment of Foot, (Mackay's Highlanders) 1794-1802* (I. H. Mackay Scobie, Edinburgh, 1914); *Records of the Scottish Volunteer Force, 1859-1908* (J. M. Grierson, Edinburgh, 1909); "Militia, Fencible Men and Home Defence, 1660-1797," in *Scotland and War: AD 79-1918* (B. Lenman, Edinburgh, 1991); "The Loyal Erskine and Inchinnan Yeomanry, from 1802 to 1853," in *Renfrewshire Family History Society Journal #42* (Gourock, 2020).

*Territorial Soldiering in the North East of Scotland during 1759 to 1814* (John Malcolm Bulloch, Aberdeen, 1914) is highly recommended. It contains a muster roll of 101 Black Watch soldiers from 1790 to 1791, 80 Fraser's Highlanders from 1775 to 1783, 940 recruits for the Gordon Highlanders in 1794, a muster roll of 295 men of the Northern Fencibles from 1778 to 1783, and much more. For example, according to a muster roll of the 92nd Regiment (The Gordon Highlanders) at Castlehill Barracks in 1794–which includes name, age, height, birthplace, trade, career, and attested date–"Norman Buchanan, 22, 5 foot, 10 inches, Skye, labourer, died of his wounds on 3 February 1800, 15 May." See also Frank Adam's *The Clans, Septs, and Regiments of the Scottish Highlands* (Edinburgh, 1908 and many later editions).

List of Northern Fencibles *(courtesy of the Spalding Club)*

## Miscellaneous

***Publications.*** *A Military History of Scotland* (E. Spiers, Edinburgh, 2014) is highly recommended. Other publications include *Uniforms of the Scottish Infantry, 1740-1900* (W. A. Thorburn, Edinburgh, 1970); *The British Army; Its History, Tradition and Records* (I. Swinnerton, Birmingham, 1996); *The Naming and Numbering of Scottish Regiments of Foot, Cavalry and Militia* (David Webster, 2002); *The Scottish Regiments* (D. Henderson, Glasgow, 1993, 1996); *Scottish Soldiers in Colonial America* (David Dobson, Baltimore, 1997-2018); *Scottish Soldiers in Europe and America, 1600-1700* (David Dobson, Baltimore, 2001); *Scottish Soldiers in Continental Europe* (David Dobson, St. Andrews, 1997); *Scottish Soldiers, 1600-1800* (David Dobson, St. Andrews, 1997), which lists Scottish soldiers for whom there are wills or testaments confirmed in Scotland; *History of the Scots Brigade in the Service of the United Netherlands, 1572-1782*, three volumes (Edinburgh, 1899-1901), which contains lists of Scottish soldiers who married and had their children baptized in the Low Countries.

## Regimental Museums

Army personnel records are in the National Archives in London; however, regimental museums contain substantial archival material, maps, diaries, muster rolls, histories of campaigns, etc., as well as weapons, uniforms, and miscellaneous artifacts. The main sources concerned with Scottish regiments are as follows:

*   The Highlanders Museum, Fort George, Ardesier, Inverness IV2.7TD; www.thehighlandersmuseum.com/ (contains collections relating to the Queen's Own Highlanders, Seaforth Highlanders, Queen's Own Cameron Highlanders, Lovat Scots, and more)

*   Gordon Highlanders Museum, St. Luke's, Viewfield Rd, Aberdeen AB15 7XH; www.gordonhighlanders.com/ (material dating from 1794)

*   The Royal Scots Fusiliers material from 1678 in the National Army Museum, Royal Hospital Rd, Chelsea, London SW3 4HT; www.nam.ac.uk/

- The Argyll and Sutherland Highlanders Museum, The Castle, Stirling FK8 1EH; www.argylls.co.uk/ (under construction at the time of this writing)

- The Cameronians (Scottish Rifles), 1689-1968, 129 Muir St, Hamilton ML3 6BJ; www.sllccameronians.co.uk/

- The Black Watch (Royal Highland Regiment) Castle and Museum, Balhousie Castle, Hay Street, Perth PH1 5HR; https://theblackwatch.co.uk/ (dates from 1739)

- The Royal Scots Dragoon Guards Museum, Edinburgh Castle, Edinburgh EH1 2YT; www.scotsdgmuseum.com/

- The King's Own Scottish Borderers Museum, The Barracks Parade, Berwick-upon-Tweed TD15 1DG; www.kosb.co.uk/museum/ (dates from 1690)

# THE JACOBITES, 1689-1746

There is substantial material in print listing those who supported the attempts to return the House of Stuart to the thrones of England, Scotland, and Ireland. Support for the Jacobites existed throughout the British Isles, but this list concentrates on Scotland and lists of participants. Their failure contributed to emigration, both voluntary and enforced, from Scotland, especially to the Americas in the eighteenth century.

*Publications*. *The Jacobite Cess Roll for the County of Aberdeen in 1715* (A. and H. Tayler, Aberdeen, 1932); *The Jacobites of Aberdeen and Banff in the Rising of 1715* (A. M. Taylor, Aberdeen, 1934); *The Jacobite Peerage* (Marquis of Auvigny, Edinburgh, 1984); *The Jacobite Risings of 1715 and 1745* (R. C. Jarvis, Cumberland, 1954); *The Forfarshire or Lord Ogilvy's Regiment* (J. R. Mackintosh, Inverness, 1914); *Jacobites of Perthshire, 1745* (Frances McDonnell, Baltimore, 1999); *Jacobites of North East Scotland, 1715 and 1745* (Frances McDonnell, Baltimore, 1997); *Jacobites of Lowland Scotland, England, Ireland, France and Spain, 1745* (Frances McDonnell, Baltimore, 2000); *Highland Jacobites, 1745*, two volumes, (Frances McDonnell, St. Andrews, 2000); *Atholl in the Rebellion of 1745* (James I. Robertson, Aberfeldy, 1994); *The Itinerary of Prince Charles*

*Edward Stuart, 1745-1746* (Walter Blaikie, Edinburgh, 1897); *The Jacobite Attempt of 1719* (William Kirk Dickson, Edinburgh, 1895); *A List of Persons Concerned in the Rebellion* (The Earl of Rosebery, Edinburgh, 1890); *The Jacobite Clans of the Great Glen from 1650 to 1784* (Bruce Lenman, London, 1984); *The Jacobites of the '15* (David Dobson, Aberdeen, 1993); *The Jacobites of Angus, 1689-1746*, in two parts (David Dobson, St. Andrews, 1995; Baltimore,1997).

Another publication by David Dobson is *The Scottish Jacobites of 1715 and the Jacobite Diaspora* (Baltimore, 2017); entries include:

> George Keith, born 1694, son of William Keith the Earl
> Marischal, fought at Sheriffmuir in 1715, had his estates
> forfeited to the Crown as a rebel in 1715, escaped to
> France, died in Potsdam, Prussia, on 18 May 1778, also
> Alexander Gordon, a farmer in Cushnie, Aberdeenshire,
> a Jacobite who was captured and transported aboard the
> Friendship bound for Virginia on 24 May 1716, landed
> in Maryland in August 1716.

Other publications of interest include *The '45 and After* (NRS, Edinburgh, 1995), which gives an authoritative account of the historical background, with documentary extracts; *A Jacobite Source List* (NRS, Edinburgh, 1995), a recommended source that contains abstracts of documents in the NRS relating to the Jacobite Rebellions, such as the return of the Earl of Panmure's Jacobite Regiment of 1715 (NRS. GD45.1.201) and lists of men delivering up their arms upon oath, 1716 (NRS.SC54.22.51-52); *No Quarter Given* (A. Livingstone, Aberdeen, 1984; Glasgow, 2001), which contains the Muster Roll of Prince Charles Edward Stuart's Army, 1745-1746; *Sheriffmuir 1715, the Jacobite War in Scotland* (Stuart Reid, Barnsley, 2014), containing details of the Jacobite Regiments and some of their officers, also the Government Forces, plus a list of gentlemen brought as prisoners to Stirling Castle on 14 November 1715; *The Lyon in Mourning*, three volumes (Henry Paton, Edinburgh, 1896), a collection of speeches, letters, journals, etc. relative to Prince Charles Edward Stuart; "The Resolve of the Landowners of Argyllshire," a listing of the heritors of the county at Inveraray resolving to oppose any Jacobite invasion, dated August 1715 (in *The Scottish Antiquary*, vol. xiii,

Edinburgh, 1890, pages 126-129); "A list of rebel prisoners held at Inverness, 1746" (in *The Scottish Antiquary*, vol. vi, Edinburgh, 1892, pages 127-130); *The Inhabitants of the Inner Isles, Morvern and Ardnamurchan, in 1716* (Nicholas Maclean-Bristol, Edinburgh, 1998; based on NRS. SC54.22.54), which identifies the male residents, whether they fought as Jacobites or in the government militia during the 1715 Rising; *Culloden and the '45* (Jeremy Black, New York, 1990); *The Jacobite Cause* (Bruce Lenman, Edinburgh, 1986); *Prisoners of the '45*, three volumes (Bruce G. Seton and Jean G. Arnot, Edinburgh, 1928-1929).

*Records in Museums, Archives, and Libraries.* There is a considerable amount of Jacobite-related material in museums, archives, and libraries in Scotland. The National Library of Scotland has, among much other source material, "The Names of Roman Catholics, non-jurors, and others who refused to take the Oath of Allegiance in 1746" (London, 1746). The NRS has the Forfeited Estate Papers, which identify the landowners whose estates had been forfeited to the Crown due to their participation in the Jacobite Cause. These papers identify the families involved, their lands, those who rented farms from them, debtors and creditors, and correspondence. A. H. Millar's *Scottish Forfeited Estates, 1715 and 1746* (Edinburgh, 1909) and Annette M. Smith's *Jacobite Estates of the Forty-Five* (Edinburgh, 1982) are particularly useful publications about these estates.

# EDUCATION

## Universities

The universities of Scotland were established in the late medieval period and in the early modern period. By the mid-seventeenth century there were five universities in Scotland, one in St. Andrews (1413), two in Aberdeen (1495), one in Glasgow (1451), and one in Edinburgh (1592).

*Publications.* ABERDEEN: *Fasti Academiae Mariscallanae Aberdonensis, 1593-1860*, three volumes (Aberdeen,1860); *Officers and Graduates of University and King's College, Aberdeen, 1495-1860* (Aberdeen, 1893);

*Roll of Alumni in Arts of the University and King's College of Aberdeen,
1596-1860* (Aberdeen, 1900); *Records of Marischal College* (P. J. Anderson, Aberdeen, 1898); *Viri Illustrates Universitas Aberdonensis* (Aberdeen,
1932); *Alumni and Graduates in Arts in the Aberdeen Colleges, 1840-1849*
(Frances McDonnell, St. Andrews, 1995); *Alumni and Graduates in Arts
of the Aberdeen Colleges, 1850-1860* (Frances McDonnell, St. Andrews,
1996); *Roll of Graduates of the University of Aberdeen, 1860-1900* (William Johnston, Aberdeen, 1906), which contains listings such as the
following:

> James Mackay, born Inverness on 5 August 1820, son
> of George Mackay, graduated MA from King's College,
> Aberdeen, in 1840, ordained Deacon by the Bishop of
> Connecticut in 1845, a priest in 1846, incumbent of
> St. John's Episcopal Church, Inverness, 1848-1856. An
> assistant chaplain in Bengal from 1857-1875, chaplain of
> the Anglican Church in Paris from 1878 to 1887.

GLASGOW: *The Matriculation Albums of the University of Glasgow,
1727-1897* (Glasgow, 1898); *Memorials of the Faculty of Physicians and
Surgeons of Glasgow, 1599-1850* (Glasgow, 1896); *Roll of the Graduates of
the University of Glasgow from 1727 to 1897* (W. Innes Addison, Glasgow,
1898), an example from which follows:

> Benjamin Watts King, graduated MD from Glasgow
> University in 1799, sometime a practitioner in the
> West Indies, afterwards in Glasgow, died there in 1841.
> Andrew King, born 1793 in Glasgow, graduated MA
> from Glasgow University in 1812, possibly a minister in
> Torpichen and later in Glasgow, Professor of Theology
> in the Presbyterian College of Halifax, Nova Scotia, died
> in 1874. Francis Kiernan, eldest son of Fergus Kiernan
> a farmer in the parish of Killishandra, County Cavan,
> Ireland, matriculated at Glasgow University in 1769 and
> graduated MA there in 1771.

ST. ANDREWS: *Early Records of the University of St. Andrews: the Graduate Roll, 1413-1579, and the Matriculation Roll, 1473-1579* (Edinburgh,
1926); *The Matriculation Roll of the University of St. Andrews, 1747-1897*
(Edinburgh, 1905); *Biographical Register of the University of St. Andrews,*

*1747-1897* (Robert N. Smart, St. Andrews, 2004), which includes the following:

> Benjamin Franklin, born 17 January 1706 son of Joseph
> Franklin, soap boiler in Boston, and Abiah Folger, a
> printer, publisher politician and physicist, graduated
> LL.D from St. Andrews on 12 February 1759, died on 17
> April 1790; Peter Ferguson, student 1820-1821, possibly
> from Bridge of Teith, a theology student of the Secession
> Church 1824-1828, a Gaelic missionary in Canada in
> 1830.

EDINBURGH: *Calendar of the Graduates of Edinburgh* (Edinburgh, 1858); *List of the Graduates of the University of Edinburgh from 1859 to 1888* (Edinburgh, 1889); *History of the Royal College of Physicians of Edinburgh* (Oxford, 1976), which includes lists from 1681 to 1975; *The Medical Society of Edinburgh* (Edinburgh, 1850); *The Royal College of Surgeons of Edinburgh, 1581-1873* (Edinburgh, 1874); *List of the Graduates in Medicine in the University of Edinburgh, from 1705 to 1866* (Edinburgh, 1867), which tells us that although the majority of students came to the university from the British Isles, a number came from the colonies; for example, "John Moultrie, from America, graduated in medicine in 1749, while Charles Moore, from Pennsylvania, graduated in medicine in 1752."

## SCHOOLS

In the medieval period the Church began to establish choir schools and grammar schools in Scotland. Glasgow High School dates from 1124, while Dundee High School was founded in 1239. The 1496 Education Acts decreed that landowners should send their sons to study Latin, the arts, and law, thus making education compulsory, at least for the sons of the elite. Girls could also attend schools. One of the aims of the Reformers in the mid-sixteenth century was to establish a school in every parish, an aim that was generally achieved, though it happened later in the Gaelic-speaking areas of the Highlands due to the lack of Gaelic-speaking graduates. In 1811 the Edinburgh Society for the Support of Gaelic Schools was founded, with the aim of spreading Evangelical Christianity through teaching Gaelic speakers to read the Bible. (NB:

It was not until 1767 that the New Testament was available in Scottish Gaelic, and not until 1801 for the Old Testament.) In the main burghs there were Grammar or High Schools with wider curriculums.

**Publications.** During the nineteenth century several fee-paying schools were founded, and it is their records that are most available in print. These include *Aberdeen Grammar School, Roll of Pupils, 1795-1919* (Aberdeen, 1923); *Chanonry House School, Aberdeen, Pupil Roll 1843-1879* (Aberdeen, 1923); *Aberdeen Grammar School, Roll of Pupils from 1795 to 1919* (Theodore Watt, Aberdeen, 1923), which includes listings such as the following:

> William W. Aberdein, entered aged 14, of 25 Ferryhill Place, a pupil 1879-1880, for over 20 years employed as a bookkeeper in New York city, died there on 1 October 1909. James Allan, of Crown Street, Aberdeen, entered aged 14, a pupil 1869 to 1872, went to America many years ago.

*The Morgan. Its Origins and History, 1868-2018* (Rodger J. H. Brunton, Dundee, 2017); *The Cargilfield Register, Edinburgh, 1873-1927* (Edinburgh, 1928); *The Loretto Register, 1825-1948* (Edinburgh, 1949); *Edinburgh Academy Register from 1814* (Edinburgh 1914); *George Watson's College, 1724-1970* (Edinburgh 1900); *Fettes College in Edinburgh, Register, 1870-1932* (Edinburgh, 1933); *Merchiston Castle School Registers, 1832-1962* (Edinburgh, 1962); *The Schools and Schoolmasters of Falkirk* (James Love, Falkirk, 1898); *Glasgow Academy, 1846-1946* (Glasgow, 1946); *The Glenalmond Register, 1847-1954* (Glenalmond,1955), the first entry of which follows:

> Henry Reid Bell, born 29 May 1832, son of Captain W. Bell of the Bengal Horse Artillery, a pupil at Glenalmond in 1847-1848, a cadet of the Madras Native Infantry in 1849, an Ensign of the 25th Madras Native Infantry in 1849, a Lieutenant in 1855, retired in 1858, Inspector of Police in Mauritius in 1862, Police Magistrate at Rodriguez in 1871, Superintendent of Prisons at Port Louis in 1879, Superintendent of Police in Mauritius in 1882, retired in 1889, went to farm in New Zealand, died at Manutahi, Taranaki, New Zealand, on 26 October 1902.

*St. Leonard's School, Register,* volume 1, 1877-1895, volume 2, 1895-1900 (St. Andrews, 1895-1901); *Scottish Schoolmasters of the Seventeenth Century* (David Dobson, St. Andrews, 1995); and *The Society in Scotland for Propagating Christian Knowledge Schoolmasters from 1709 to 1872* (the society had 323 schools in 1795, mostly in the Highlands and Island, and its schoolmasters included "Alexander Cameron, at Kilmanivaig in 1726, at Ratalichmore from 1729 to 1731, in Drumfuir in 1737, Lanachan from 1738 to 1739, died there").

The vast majority of pupils in Scotland attended the local parish schools, which were mainly in the hands of the Church of Scotland, the rest being Episcopalian or Roman Catholic. The churches' responsibility for schools began to diminish during the nineteenth century and, beginning in 1872, the State became increasingly involved.

***Records in Archives.*** School records, generally administrative and financial, have survived in local archives. Admission registers exist but are far from comprehensive, and there are restrictions on access to those less than 100 years old. Take the case of Dundee City Archives, which has a substantial collection of school records. For the local Industrial Schools, there are admission registers for girls from 1855 to 1924 (DCA.GD/Balg/2/3/1-6) and for boys, 1855 to 1878, and from 1873 to 1980 (DCA.GD/Balg/3/3/1-9); Dundee High School admission registers for boys from 1880 to 1904 and girls from 1902 to 1904; Harris Academy admissions registers from 1885 to 1919; Hawkhill School admission registers from 1869 to 1887; and Drumgeith School admission registers from 1874 to 1914.

Edinburgh City Archives has the records of the Royal High School from 1763 to 1993 (ECA.SL137); Slateford School from 1864 to 1924 (ECA.SL211); Dean Free Church School from 1868 to 1886 (ECA.SL181); and Duncan Place School from 1864 to 1892 (ECA.SL185). Highland Archives has education records from the 1860s, including admission registers, such as those for Grantown Female School from 1862 to 1890 (HA.CM.5.6.1).

Sign indicating place of care for the poor *(courtesy of the Moray District Council)*

## POOR LAW RECORDS

During the early modern period, relief of the poor in Scotland was the responsibility of the Church of Scotland. The records of such support are recorded in the Kirk Session Records of the various parishes, mostly deposited in the NRS. Each parish was responsible for their poor, who were eligible by birth, marriage, and length of residence. The sick and disabled, but not the unemployed, were eligible for help, possibly in a poorhouse. By the early Victorian period, this system was replaced by a state-sponsored program. Inspectors of the Poor kept detailed records of the individuals claiming support. These records, many of which survive, provide names, dates of birth, places of birth, religion, children, marital state, etc.

**Publications.** *The Scottish Poor Law: Its Operation in the North East from 1745 to 1845* (J. O. Lindsay, Ilfracombe, 1975) and *The Old Poor Law in Scotland: The Experience of Poverty from 1574 to 1845* (R. Mitchison, Edinburgh, 2000).

**Records in Archives.** The situation changed in 1845 with the Poor Law Amendment Act, which established Parochial Poor Relief Boards. The best collection of Poor Relief Records can be found in the Glasgow City Archives. They contain the name, age, birthplace, applicant's marital history, and whether the applicant was a pauper or not. The Glasgow City Archives has records for Glasgow from 1851 to 1948, Barony from 1861 to 1898, and Govan from 1876 to 1930, as well as records mostly dating from 1845 for Bute, Dunbartonshire, Lanarkshire, and Renfrewshire.

Ayrshire Archives also has application records for most parishes, as do Lanarkshire, Renfrewshire and Dunbartonshire. The records for Aberdeen, Banff, Kincardine, and Moray can be consulted in Aberdeen City Archives' Old Aberdeen House office. Aberdeen City Archives also has the records of St. Nicholas Poorhouse from 1779 to 1788.

Dundee City Archives has substantial administrative records pertaining to the local poorhouse as well as the General Register of the East Poorhouse between 1856 and 1878. This Register (DCA.Acc1978/0063) gives dates of admission, name, age, place of birth, length of residence in parish, religion, trade, disease, cause of death, conduct, and name of chargeable parish. The Archives also holds the records of the neighboring parish of Liff and Benvie, including the Register of Poor admitted to the parochial poorhouse between 1854 and 1865 (DCA.Acc1981/0023).

Edinburgh City Archives has the Canongate Charity Workhouse records from 1761 to 1874 (ECA.SL11); Craiglockhart Poorhouse records from

1859 to 1963 (ECA.SL9); Edinburgh Charity Workhouse records from 1739 to 1849 (ECA.SL146); and St. Cuthbert/West Kirk records from 1762 to 1862 (ECA.SL222). Paisley Heritage Centre has the Renfrewshire Poor Law Records from 1839 to 1948.

# THE REGISTER OF THE PRIVY COUNCIL OF SCOTLAND

The Register of the Privy Council of Scotland contained the records of a committee set up to advise the monarch on a wide range of subjects—political, economic, social, and administrative—and is therefore a potential treasure trove for family historians. The Register functioned from 1545 until the Union of Parliaments in 1707. It has been largely published in a multi-volumed series from 1545 until 1689; the subsequent years exist in manuscripts in the National Records of Scotland in Edinburgh.

*Publications.* The published volumes are well indexed and partly in English, so you can find people or events quite easily. There are references to trade and shipping, witches, banishment, recusants, Covenanters, Jacobites, and lawlessness in the Highlands and on the Borders. The published volumes can be found in major reference libraries, such as the National Library of Scotland. They have been digitized and are viewable online at **https://catalog.hathitrust.org/Record/010426810**. People at every level of society in Scotland are mentioned. It is a source that should not be overlooked for the early modern period.

# PRISONERS

Edinburgh had its own jail or tolbooth, which acted as a national prison, while the nearby burghs of Canongate and Leith had their own tolbooths, where many prisoners were kept before being shipped to the colonies—not only felons like Agnes Bayne, banished to Barbados in 1663, but also political or religious rebels, mainly Covenanters, such as Robert Goodwin, who was bound for East New Jersey in 1685.

**Publications.** Details of those being banished in the seventeenth century can be found in the published Register of the Privy Council of Scotland (see previous page for the URL to view this Register). Also see the Edinburgh Tolbooth Records from 1657 to 1816, which were partly published in the volumes of the *Book of the Old Edinburgh Club* (full views of some volumes of this publication and limited views of others are available at **https://catalog.hathitrust.org/Record/000063100**). Entries include listings like the following:

> On 10 October 1657, Janet Bruce, having been found guilty of witchcraft was to be taken on 14 October1657 to the Castlehill and strangled until dead, then her body was to be burnt to ashes.

David Dobson's *Directory of Scots Banished to the American Plantations, 1650-1775*, second edition (Baltimore, 2010), lists criminals, Covenanters, and Jacobite prisoners of war who were transported to the colonies for sale during the colonial period; for example,

> James Forrest, a Covenanter from Cambusnethan, Lanarkshire, who was banished on 24 July 1685, then transported from Leith in August 1685 bound for Jamaica, landed at Port Royal on 7 December 1685.

Relevant publications include *They Did Wrong. Public Hangings in the Angus area, 1785-1868* (Jessie Sword, Dundee, 2005) and *A Handlist of Records for the Study of Crime in Early Modern Scotland to 1747* (Bruce Lenman, London, 1982); and *Fife Convict Transportees, 1752 to 1867* (Andrew J. Campbell, Kirkcaldy, 1995), which deals mainly with prisoners sent to Australia.

Newspapers and journals, such as the *Aberdeen Journal* and the *Edinburgh Evening Courant*, regularly reported on trials. Possibly the best such source is the *Scots Magazine*, especially for the period between 1739 and 1826, where reports on trials and punishments were regular features. For example, it reported on the Jacobite Rebellion throughout 1745 and 1746 and the subsequent trials of Jacobite prisoners.

*Records in Archives.* The NRS contains records of prisoners from all over Scotland since the middle of the seventeenth century, which provide the details of trials, sentences, place of birth of the accused, age, height, occupation, and religion (NRS.HH.21). There are also prison registers for the following counties: Angus from 1805 to 1827, Ayr from 1860 to 1863, Jedburgh from 1839 to 1893, Kirkcudbright from 1791 to 1811, Selkirk from 1828 to 1840, and Stirling from 1822 to 1829.

# MENTAL HEALTH RECORDS

*Records in Archives.* The NRS has the Notice of Admissions by the Superintendent of Mental Institutions from 1858 to 1962 (NRS.MC2). The Scottish Indexes "Mental Health Records in Scotland" website **(www.scottishindexes.com/learninghealth.aspx#q3)** says, "This is arguably the most interesting record relating to people with mental health problems that you will find in the National Records of Scotland. The reason we would make this statement is that as well as giving detailed information about the patient, it gives such information as the "Supposed Cause" of their illness, observations of the patient by two physicians, and accounts regarding the patient that the physician was told by people who knew the individual concerned. Also in the NRS is the General Register of Lunatics in Asylums from 1805 until 1962 (NRS.MC7.33.1).

Edinburgh City Archives has the records of the Magdalene Asylum from 1798 to 1938 (ECA.SL237). Highland Archives has the records of Inverness District Asylum from 1849 to 2002, including patients registers from 1864 to 1995.

St. Andrews, from the beach, Edinburgh, Scotland *(courtesy of Marian and Brent Hoffman)*

Chapter 5
# EMIGRATION

There has been significant emigration, both in absolute and relative terms, from Scotland since the medieval period. Relative to their population, the Scots have one of the highest rates of emigration in Europe—only surpassed by the Irish and the Norwegians. One estimate suggests that up to 30,000,000 people worldwide are of Scottish origin. Genealogists and family historians are particularly keen to establish their Scottish origins. Most Americans and Canadians of Scottish origin are descended from people who moved directly from Scotland, but there is a minority whose ancestors were two-stage migrants arriving via the West Indies, Ireland, or some other European country. So it is vital to know the destinations of many migrants before they, or their descendants, landed in North America.

Initially, the main destinations of emigrants from Scotland were locations along the Baltic Sea and the North Sea, places with which Scotland had trading connections, especially Scandinavia, Poland, the Netherlands, and France. Ireland, mainly Ulster, became the most important destination for Scots emigrants during the seventeenth century; by 1700 there were about 100,000 Scots settled there. Their descendants, the "Scotch-Irish," became the single most numerous immigrant group to settle in colonial America during the eighteenth century.

# SCOTS IN THE NETHERLANDS

Scottish scholars and merchants had long been attracted by the opportunities available in the universities and cities of Holland, Zeeland, and
Flanders. Scottish students—who, prior to the establishment of universities in Scotland during the fifteenth century, had either to study in
England or on the continent—were attracted by courses in law and medicine offered by the Dutch universities. Scottish merchants and craftsmen
could be found in towns and cities throughout the Low Countries, notably in Veere, Middelburg, Amsterdam, and Rotterdam. Antwerp, and
later Rotterdam, were the great emporiums of northern Europe, where
colonial produce from America, Africa, and Asia was distributed.

During the seventeenth century Scots communities, with their own
churches, could be found throughout Holland, and in Zeeland in particular, and by 1700 about one thousand Scots lived in Rotterdam alone.
Some of the Scots found in the Netherlands were religious or political
refugees, such as the Covenanters who fled persecution under the Stuart
kings to live among their Calvinist brethren. Many Scots found in the
Netherlands in the early modern period were soldiers fighting in the service of the United Provinces against the Spanish Hapsburgs. The Netherlands were once under the overlordship of the Hapsburg Empire, but
the Reformation of the sixteenth century led to the northern provinces
breaking away. For eighty years the Dutch fought to maintain their independence and aiding them in their struggle with Spain were thousands
of Scottish soldiers who formed the Scots Brigade. The Scots Brigade was
established in 1572 and remained in Dutch service until 1782; many of
the soldiers married and settled in the Netherlands. Some of them and
their descendants immigrated to the Dutch settlements in the Americas,
stretching from the Hudson River to Surinam.

*Publications*. *Scotland and the Low Countries, 1124-1994* (Grant G.
Simpson, East Linton, 1996); *Scotland and the Flemish People* (Alexander
Fleming and Roger Mason, Edinburgh, 2019); "Scots along the Maas,
1570-1750" (D. Catterall in *Scottish Communities Abroad in the Early
Modern Period*, A. Grosjean and Steve Murdoch, Leiden, 2005); "A
Haven for Intrigue: the Scottish Exile Community in the Netherlands,

1660-1690" (Ginny Gardner in *Scottish Communities Abroad in the Early Modern Period*, A. Grosjean and Steve Murdoch, Leiden, 2005); "Scottish Students in the Netherlands, 1680-1730" (Esther Mijers in *Scottish Communities Abroad in the Early Modern Period*, A. Grosjean and Steve Murdoch, Leiden, 2005).

## SCOTS IN SCANDINAVIA

During the sixteenth and seventeenth centuries there was significant emigration, both permanent and temporary, from Scotland to the Scandinavian lands of Norway, Sweden, and Denmark. Some of this was by economic migrants, especially merchants and craftsmen, in search of career opportunities, but most Scots went as soldiers-of-fortune seeking employment in the armies of Sweden and Norway-Denmark, particularly under the monarchy of Gustavus Adolphus, King of Sweden. Recent research indicates that between 1627 and 1629, around 13,700 Scots entered Danish service, and that in 1631 there were 20,000 Scots in Swedish service. Many of those who arrived as soldiers and survived campaigns, especially the Thirty Years War, were granted land and encouraged to settle. In 1638, on the outbreak of the Bishops War, the start of the Wars of the Three Kingdoms, many of the Scottish soldiers returned from Scandinavia to form the backbone of the Covenanter Army that successfully opposed the forces of King Charles I.

The Swedish and Danish kings not only recruited soldiers from Scotland but also seafarers. Experienced seafarers were employed in various capacities; for example, John Cunningham from Crail led a Danish naval expedition to Greenland and Labrador in 1605. Later he became governor of Vardohu and Finmark in northern Norway. Several of the admirals of the Swedish Navy belonged to the Scottish Clerck family. Sanders Clerck took part in the Swedish expedition to the Delaware in 1639, while Richard Clerck acted as commissary to the Swedish West India Company around 1646.

The merchants and craftsmen who immigrated to Scandinavia generally originated from burghs along the east coast of Scotland, as far north as the Orkney and Shetland Islands. There were also important trading links between Scottish east-coast ports and Norwegian ports, such as Bergen, Trondheim, Stavanger, and Christiansand; Swedish ports such as Gothenburg and Stockholm; and to a lesser extent, Copenhagen in Denmark, which led to merchants, factors, and craftsmen settling in those places.

The failure of the Jacobites in 1715 and 1746 caused a number of Jacobites to seek refuge in Sweden; some, such as the Carnegies, became burghers of Gothenburg, which had attracted Scottish immigrants since the city was developed in the seventeenth century. It was the home to the Swedish East India Company, which was created around 1730 to rival the English and the Dutch East India Companies. One of its more prominent employees was Colin Campbell, who was sent to China in 1731 to establish trading links. The industrialization of Gothenburg in the nineteenth century was facilitated by Scottish entrepreneurs such as James Dickson, William Dickson, and Alexander Keiller. During the early modern period, tens of thousands of Scots settled in Scandinavia, some permanently and others temporarily. Some of them, or their descendants, were involved in trade and settlement in the Americas. Several Scots were recorded as planters and merchants in the Danish West Indian colony of the Virgin Islands—St. Jan (St. John), St. Thomas, and St. Croix—during the eighteenth and nineteenth centuries.

***Publications***. *Scots-Scandinavian Links in Europe and America, 1550-1850*, second edition (David Dobson, Baltimore, 2020); "Scottish Immigration to Bergen in the Sixteenth and Seventeenth Centuries" (N. O. Pedersen in *Scottish Communities Abroad in the Early Modern Period*, A. Grosjean and Steve Murdoch, Leiden, 2005); "The Scottish Community in Seventeenth Century Gothenburg" (A. Grosjean and S. Murdoch in *Scottish Communities Abroad in the Early Modern Period*, A. Grosjean and Steve Murdoch, Leiden, 2005); *Should Auld Acquaintance Be Forgot...Scottish Danish Relations, 1450-1707*, two volumes (Thomas Riis, Odense, 1988); *Scots on Sweden* (J. Berg and B. Lagercrantz, Stockholm, 1962).

# SCOTS IN FRANCE

Since the medieval period Scotland has had strong economic and social links with France, which led to settlement there by Scots. During the medieval period many Scottish soldiers fought for France, including during the Hundred Years War between England and France. Subsequently, some of the survivors settled there; for example, Nicholas Chambers was granted the seigneury of Guerche in Tourane in 1444. Other families who settled in France included Kinnimond (as Quinemont), Gowrie (as Gohory), Douglas (as Du Glas), Drummond (as Drumont), Crawford (as de Crafort), Lockhart (as Locart), Turnbull (as Torneboule), and Ramsay (as de Ramezay).

During the early modern period France continued to attract Scottish soldiers; for example, in August 1627 two thousand Scottish soldiers under William, the 6th Earl of Morton, were despatched to France to assist the Huguenots in La Rochelle, where they were besieged. In the eighteenth century many Jacobites fled to France—men like John Erskine, born 1675, son of the Duke of Mar, who escaped to St. Malo in 1716 and died at Aix la Chapelle in 1732. Some were enrolled in French regiments—such as the *Royal Ecossois* or the *Regiment d'Ogilvie*—which were sent to support Bonnie Prince Charlie in 1745. In 1746 Jacobite prisoners of war being transported aboard the ship *Veteran* for sale as indentured servants on the Leeward Islands were liberated by a French privateer and landed on the French island of Martinique. Some of them were recruited into the local militia, while others may have gone to Bordeaux.

Economic opportunities in France attracted many Scottish merchants, who generally settled in ports such as Rouen, Dunkirk, Bordeaux, Dieppe, and Calais, while some were attracted to Paris. Before the Reformation, and to a lesser extent thereafter, the universities of France attracted scholars from Scotland. For example, Alexander Dundas graduated as an MD from Rheims University in 1695. After the Reformation, Catholic families in Scotland sent their sons to be educated at seminaries in France, such as the Scots College in Paris and in Doui. Scots could also be found in French colonies in the Americas in the early modern period; for example, Duncan McIntosh settled on Martinique in 1774.

**Publications.** *Scots-French Links in Europe and America, 1550-1850* (David Dobson, Baltimore, 2011); *Scottish Soldiers in France in the Reign of the Sun King* (M. Glozier, Boston, 2004).

# SCOTS IN POLAND-LITHUANIA

The links between Scotland and the countries lying along the southern shore of the Baltic Sea can be traced back as far as the late medieval period, when Scottish knights accompanied the Teutonic Knights on the Baltic Crusade against the heathen Letts. The Teutonic Knights established German colonies in what became East Prussia and expanded or developed numerous ports—including Memel, Konigsberg, and Danzig—which traded with countries lying to the west, including Scotland. This led to merchants, factors, and craftsmen settling in those places.

The main period of Scottish settlement along the Baltic was between 1560 and about 1650; many of the settlers were former soldiers who had fought in the armies of Poland, Russia, and Sweden. By the middle of the seventeenth century, there was hardly a district in Poland-Lithuania that did not have a Scottish presence. By the 1640s it is reckoned that there were around 30,000 Scots resident there. Religious liberty, which existed in Poland for much of the period, attracted immigrants who were subject to persecution in their homelands, such as some Catholic families from Scotland. Much of the immigration into Poland at the period arose through economic opportunity, created by the existing social structure under which society was divided between the aristocracy and the peasantry, with a socio-economic gap in between. This gap was filled mainly by German, Dutch, Scots, and Jewish entrepreneurs. By the late seventeenth century, Scottish immigration to Poland and the Baltic states diminished, as new opportunities arose, initially in Ireland and increasingly in America and the West Indies. Economic links between Scotland and the Baltic lands were maintained and expanded during the eighteenth and nineteenth centuries. The Scottish communities gradually integrated, and most Scottish surnames became unrecognizable, though a few retained their original forms, for example, John Charles Graham, who was born in Danzig in 1804 and settled in Charleston, South Carolina, in 1829.

**Publications.** *The Scots in Prussia*, six volumes (D. Richard Torrance, Edinburgh, 2014); *Scotland and Poland, Historical Encounters, 1500-2010* (T. M. Devine and D. Hesse, Edinburgh, 2011); *Ships, Guns and Bibles in the North Sea and the Baltic States* (I. MacInnes, T. Riis, and F. G. Pedersen, East Linton, 2000); *Scots in Poland, Russia, and the Baltic States, 1550-1850*, three parts (David Dobson, Baltimore, 2000, 2009, 2019); "The Scottish Community in Kedainai, 1630-1750" (R. Zirgulis, in *Scottish Communities Abroad in the Early Modern Period*, A. Grosjean & Steve Murdoch, Leiden, 2005); *The Scottish Community in the Grand Duchy of Lithuania, 1630-1750* (Michael Broun Ayre, Vilnius, 2019).

Advertisement recruiting emigrants from Scotland to Russia *(from the Edinburgh Evening Courant)*

# SCOTS IN RUSSIA

Emigration from Scotland to Russia was limited in numbers. During the early modern period Scots soldiers and sailors were recruited for service in Russia. This began around 1650 in the aftermath of the Wars of the

Three Kingdoms. One of the most famous emigrants was Patrick Gordon from Ellon, who served in the armies of Poland and Sweden before entering Russian service, where he became confidant and adviser to Peter the Great. Another was Thomas Dalzell of the Binns, who returned from a military career in Russia in 1665 to persecute the Covenanters.

Several former officers of the Royal Navy were recruited into Russian service. Samuel Greig from Inverkeithing served in the Royal Navy during the Seven Years War and joined the Russian Navy in 1764. He reached the rank of Vice Admiral and Commander of Kronstadt and died at the battle of Hogland in 1788. Scottish doctors were in demand in Russia. John Rogerson (1741-1823) from Dumfries-shire became a physician at the court of Catherine the Great. Probably the greatest Scots architect in Russia was Charles Cameron (1745-1812), who settled in St. Petersburg in 1779 as architect to Empress Catherine of Russia. He brought several Scottish stonemasons, bricklayers, and smiths with him, men such as James Wilson. James Wilson's son Alexander became director of the Alexandrovsk textile mill in St. Petersburg and mint-master of the Izhorsky ironworks in Kolpino. Scots merchants also settled in Russia, especially in St. Petersburg and also in Archangel and Narva, from which they shipped cargoes of timber and flax back to Scotland. The Carron Iron Works near Falkirk, one of the largest in Europe, supplied armaments to Russia. Catherine the Great, wishing to expand and improve her weapons factory at Petrovodsk, persuaded skilled ironworkers of the Carron Company to settle in Russia in the 1780s. Russia, therefore, attracted men with industrial skills, physicians, sailors, and soldiers, as well as merchants, albeit on a small scale.

**Publications.** *Scots in Poland, Russia, and the Baltic States, 1550-1850,* three parts (David Dobson, Baltimore, 2000, 2009, 2019); *The Caledonian Phalanx, Scots in Russia* (P. Dukes, Edinburgh, 1987).

## SCOTS IN GERMANY

Until the nineteenth century Germany did not exist as a single political unit, so Scottish links existed with certain distinct regions, which in the seventeenth and eighteenth centuries were the Duchy of Bremen-Verden, the Duchy of Holstein, the Duchy of Mecklenburg, Pomerania, East Frisia, and the City of Bremen—all bordering the North Sea or the Baltic Sea. As early as 1297 Andrew Moray and William Wallace, as Guardians of the Community of Scotland and leaders of the Army of Scotland, wrote to the magistrates and citizens of Lubeck and Hamburg, thanking them for their assistance in resisting English domination and offering them safe access to Scottish ports. However, trade between these north German city states was relatively small-scale, the emphasis of Scottish trade being with Scandinavia, the Baltic, and the Netherlands. Consequently, the settlement of Scottish merchants and their factors was limited to Hamburg, Bremen, and Lubeck, unless the old Hanseatic ports along the Baltic, such as Memel, are included.

By the seventeenth century Hamburg was the port most concerned with Scottish trade, particularly with the Shetland Islands. This trade, mainly of cod and herring, was in the hands of the Hitland (Shetland) Company of Hamburg, which employed some Scottish residents of Hamburg, men such as Laurence Sinclair in 1593 and Angus Murray in 1617. Among the Scottish merchants who settled in Hamburg was Robert Jolly from Leith between 1683 and his death in 1714. The Company of Hamburg Merchants Trading to England did occasionally call at Scottish ports, generally to buy supplies of coal, but trade directly from Scotland to Hamburg or other German ports was limited. Consequently, the number of Scots found there was minimal, though the records of the German Reformed Church in Hamburg do identify a few seventeenth-century men, such as Alexander Stevenson from St. Andrews and John Thomson from Carron. The records of the Anglican Church in Hamburg mention some people bearing distinctive Scottish names; for example, George Stewart married Magdelen Williams in 1624 and James Murray married Margaret Davidson in 1626. The Church of Scotland at that time had an Episcopalian element, which may explain why they did not marry in the Reformed Church in Hamburg. In 1630 Sir Robert Anstruther, a Scot and British diplomat, settled in Hamburg, along with his household of around twenty-five servants, said to be mainly Scottish.

The Thirty Years War brought Scottish soldiers to Germany to fight for

Gustavus Adolphus. Many landed at Bremen, Stralsund, or Hamburg. Several Scottish officers were based in Hamburg during the 1630s, including Lieutenant Colonel Robert Monro, Colonel Alexander Leslie, and General Patrick Ruthven, while Henry Monro of Fowlis died there. The outbreak of the Bishops War in Scotland in 1638—the first of the Wars of the Three Kingdoms, 1638-1651—led to arms being shipped from Hamburg to Leith for the Covenanters. The Peace of Westphalia, which ended the Thirty Years War in 1648-1649, meant that there were Scottish former soldiers in Germany. Their numbers were increased by military refugees from the Cromwellian occupation of Scotland. Some of them were then employed as military governors of towns in Germany; General Patrick More was commandant of Buxtehude from 1646 to the 1670s, while Colonel William Forbes was governor of Burg in Bremen-Verden from 1649 to 1657. Many ordinary soldiers became "cramers" or pedlars trafficking throughout Germany and Poland. Possibly the most famous soldier in German service was James Keith, 1696-1758, from Peterhead, who served as a soldier in Spain and Russia before becoming a Field Marshal under Frederick the Great of Prussia.

Apart from numerous soldiers and the relatively few merchants, there were those who settled in Germany as religious refugees. After the Reformation of 1560 in Scotland, Catholic families preferred to send their sons to seminaries or colleges on the continent—such as those in Wurzburg and Ratisbon—to be educated. For example, Robert Forbes professed at the Monastery of St. James in Wurzburg by 1614, matriculated at Wurtzburg in 1629, and served as Abbot there from 1636 to 1637. William Howie, a priest from the Diocese of Aberdeen, matriculated at the University of Koln in 1469, while Charles Fraser was at the Ratisbon Seminary in 1756. Protestant Scots also studied in Germany. Mungo Inglis, a graduate of Edinburgh University, is known to have been at Heidelberg and Hamburg before becoming a tutor at the College of William and Mary in Virginia from 1694 to 1705, while Andrew Aidie from Aberdeen studied at the University of Heidelberg around 1603 and later became Professor of Philosophy at Danzig.

Sometimes a Scot wishing to become a citizen of a German city was required to prove that he was of acceptable origins, so he would write to the magistrates of his local burgh for a birth brief. Andrew Fraser, son of Alaster Fraser of Glenshee and his wife Elspeth Spalding, a traveler in Butzoe, Mecklenburg, was granted a birth brief by the magistrates of Dundee on 13 July 1616, and James Chalmers in Silesia, son of Gilbert Chalmers and his wife Christian Con in Kintore, was granted a birth brief by Aberdeen magistrates in 1700.

*Publications*. "Britannia ist Mein Patria: Scotsmen and the British Community in Hamburg" (K. Zickerman, in *Scottish Communities Abroad in the Early Modern Period*, A. Grosjean and Steve Murdoch, Leiden, 2005); *The Scots in Germany* (Thomas A. Fischer, Edinburgh, 1902); *The Scots in Prussia*, six volumes (D. R. Torrance, Edinburgh, 2014); *Scottish-German Links, 1550-1850*, second edition (David Dobson. Baltimore, 2011); *Across the German Sea: Early Modern Scottish Connections with the Wider Elbe-Weser Region* (K. Zickerman, Leiden, 2013).

# SCOTS IN SOUTHERN EUROPE

The countries of southern Europe attracted relatively few immigrants from Scotland in the early modern period. Those Scots found in areas such as Spain or Italy in the sixteenth, seventeenth, and eighteenth centuries were predominantly Roman Catholics; for example, many sons of Scottish Catholic families were sent to colleges in Spain, Italy, or France to complete their education—most were destined for the priesthood, including Robert Callendar, a student at the Scots College in Rome around 1617, later a missionary in Scotland. The failure of the Jacobite Rebellions of 1715 and 1745 resulted in a number of Jacobites taking refuge within Catholic Europe, especially in Italy where the Court of King James Stuart was based. Other Jacobite refugees became merchants, often in the wine trade (notably, members of the Gordon clan), in locations such as Madeira, Cadiz, Xerez, and Lisbon.

By the eighteenth century aristocratic families often sent their sons on the Grand Tour of Europe, especially to Italy and Greece; subsequently, Scottish artists and scholars settled there, some permanently, others temporarily. The expansion of the British Empire during the eighteenth and nineteenth centuries led to Scottish soldiers and sailors being stationed at places such as Gibraltar and Malta, while the Iberian Campaign of the Napoleonic Wars brought many Scottish fighting men to Spain and Portugal, mostly in British service but some in Portuguese service, such as General David Calder in the service of the King of Portugal around 1784. Scottish settlement around the Mediterranean was small-scale and mainly composed of military personnel, merchants, scholars, artists, and those attracted by the climate.

**Publications.** *Scots in Southern Europe, 1600-1900*, second edition (David Dobson, Baltimore, 2019); *British Residents and Their Problems in Madeira Before 1815* (W. Minchinton, Funchal, 1989).

# SCOTS IN IRELAND

There had been migration between Scotland and Ireland in the medieval period, but the seventeenth century was the period of greatest settlement of Scots in Ireland. The English kings had attempted for centuries to rule and control Ireland, with varying degrees of success. In the Middle Ages mercenary soldiers from the Highlands and Islands, the *Galloglagh,* went to aid the indigenous Irish against the English in Ireland. Similarly, around 1570 approximately one thousand mercenaries ("redshanks") arrived mainly from Argyll to settle primarily in Tyrone and to fight for the Gaelic chiefs against the Tudor incomers. These Highlanders, however, had much in common with the native Irish in language, culture, and religion, unlike the Lowland Scots who arrived in Ulster during the seventeenth century.

Ulster was the last Irish province to surrender to the English. The Nine Years War ended when Queen Elizabeth's army defeated the forces of Hugh O'Neill and Hugh O'Donnell. The Flight of the (Irish) Earls to France, later Rome, in 1607 meant that their lands were forfeited to the Crown, namely James Stuart, King of Scotland, by then also King of England. From about 1570 there had been attempts to develop an English settlement in County Down, which had been foiled by the actions of the Clandeboye O'Neills. However, in 1605 King James granted one-third of the lands of Conn O'Neill to two Ayrshire landowners, Sir Hugh Montgomery and James Hamilton. They soon brought settlers from their lands in Lowland Scotland. The largest land grant made in Ulster in the early seventeenth century was made to Randal MacDonnell, whose family had originated in the Western Isles of Scotland. This was surprising, as MacDonnell was a practicing Roman Catholic; however, he did import Lowland Protestants to settle on his lands. Further west in Ulster was George Montgomery, Protestant Bishop of Derry, Raphoe, and Clogher, who encouraged Scottish settlement on land owned by the Church.

The official Plantation of Ulster involved the counties of Armagh, Cavan, Coleraine (that is Londonderry), Donegal, Fermanagh, and Tyrone. Settlement was not restricted to the Scots but was also available to English entrepreneurs. Nine precincts were allocated to Scottish "undertakers," men who undertook to develop the land and settle British people there. By 1619 it is reckoned there were about 6,500 Scots settled on the six planted counties. Scots could also be found in locations not originally allocated to Scottish undertakers; for example, Sir Robert McClelland from Kirkcudbright leased land originally granted to London companies near Londonderry and settled them with people from Dumfries and Galloway. Overall, the vast majority of Scottish settlers in Ulster came from the counties of Ayr, Lanark, Renfrew, Dumfries, and Galloway. King James also took the opportunity to rid the Borders of families of "reivers," who had been lawless for generations; most of them—Armstrongs, Johnstons, Elliots, and Grahams—were settled in County Fermanagh. Initially, most Scottish settlers engaged in farming, but there were a number of towns established and settled by tradesmen and settlers. The majority of Scots immigrants to Ulster were Protestant, some were Episcopalian, others Presbyterian, with a few Roman Catholics. The leading Scottish families settling during the Plantation of Ulster were the Hamiltons, Montgomerys, Edmonstones, Agnews, Shaws, Colvilles, Adairs, MacDonnells, Stewarts, McClellands, Achesons, Richardsons, Erskines, Drummonds, Humes, Dunbars, Murrays, Knoxs, Cunninghams, Leslies, Balfours, Crichtons, and Baillies. Scottish immigration to Ulster continued throughout the seventeenth century and into the early eighteenth century. By 1700 there were around 100,000 Scots and their descendants settled in the north of Ireland. Migration from Scotland, which had been directed at Ireland for over a century, now had a new target. Beginning in about 1718, there was significant emigration of Protestants from Ulster to the Americas, where they became the third largest immigrant group of the colonial period.

**Publications.** "Scottish Migration to Ireland in the Seventeenth Century" (Patrick Fitzgerald, in *Scottish Communities Abroad in the Early Modern Period*, A. Grosjean and Steve Murdoch, Leiden, 2005); *Scotland and the Ulster Plantations* (W. Kelly and J. R. Young, Dublin, 2009); *The Scottish Migration to Ulster in the Reign of James* I (M. Percival-Maxwell, London, 1973); *Scots-Irish Links, 1575-1725*, ten parts (David Dobson, Baltimore, 1997-2017).

## SCOTS IN AUSTRALASIA

Possibly around 3,000 Scots had been shipped in chains to the American colonies to be disposed of as indentured servants there. After the American War of Independence, however, felons could no longer be transported to America, so the British government transported them mostly to Australia instead—between 1788 and 1868 about 150,000 convicts, including a number of Scots, were transported from the British Isles. By the 1830s Australia was receiving a steady flow of migrants from Scotland. The Highland Clearances, a system whereby landowners in the Highlands would evict tenant farmers from their lands and replace them with a more profitable option, the introduction of sheep, was then in full swing. The Highland and Islands Emigration Society was established to facilitate the immigration of dispossessed clansmen and their families to Australia in the middle of the nineteenth century. The Highland Clearances also generated immigration to Canada from the late eighteenth century onward. The discovery of gold in California, South Africa, Australia, and New Zealand produced an increase in immigration to these locations also.

The settlement of New Zealand by the British post-dated that of Australia by a generation or two, really commencing in the 1830s. The first contingent of emigrants directly from Scotland to New Zealand occurred in 1826 with the voyage of the *Rosanna* from Leith in 1826. In the early days the majority of settlers went under the auspices of the New Zealand Company, but by the 1840s a significant proportion of organized settlement was church based, such as that at Otago by members of the Church of Scotland or by the followers of the Reverend Norman MacLeod, who arrived via Nova Scotia where they had initially settled from the Highlands. By the close of the nineteenth century, about a quarter of the population of New Zealand were Scots or of Scottish origin.

**Publications**. *Far Off in Sunlit Places: the Scots in Australia and New Zealand* (J. Hewitson, Edinburgh, 1998); *A Directory of Scots in Australasia, 1788-1900*, three parts (David Dobson, St. Andrews, 1997); *Caledonia Australia* (D. Watson, Sydney, 1984); *That Land of Exiles, Scots in Australia* (Edinburgh, 1988); *Scots in Australia, 1788-1900* (M. D. Prentis, Sydney, 1983); *The Welsh, Irish, Scots, and English in Australia* (D. Lucas, Canberra, 1987); *Scots in Australia, 1788-1988* (Edinburgh, 1988); *Scottishness and Irishness in New Zealand since 1840* (Angela McCarthy, Manchester, 2011).

## SCOTS IN LATIN AMERICA

Emigration from Scotland only began in earnest once the power of Spain in the hemisphere began to wane. In the late seventeenth century and the eighteenth century, there were locations, such as the Bay of Honduras or Surinam, where Scots planters and merchants could settle. The attempt to settle a trading colony at Darien in 1698-1699 was an expensive failure, due in part to the opposition of Spain. Many of the 3,000 Scots died there, with the survivors taking refuge in Jamaica and along the American coast from Charleston to New York. The Wars of Liberation during the early nineteenth century removed the restrictions on immigration imposed by Spain.

The end of the Napoleonic Wars in Europe in 1815 resulted in substantial numbers of demobilized sailors and soldiers, including many Scots, flocking to South America to aid the revolutionaries in their struggle for liberty from Spain. Among them was Sir Thomas Cochrane, Earl of Dundonald, who between 1818 and 1860 was Commander in Chief of the Chilean Navy and later of the Brazilian Navy. Once liberation was achieved emigration occurred, and Scottish companies began to invest in Latin America. British merchant houses, banks, railway companies, mining companies, industrialists, planters, and ranchers became established throughout Latin America, and they brought with them skilled workers and professionals from throughout the British Isles. The first direct shipment of Scots emigrants occurred in 1825 with the *Norval*, the *Symetry*, and the *Harmony* bound for Argentina with bricklayers, implement makers, blacksmiths, miners, quarriers, and farmers. That same year the *Planet of London* sailed from Cromarty with a shipload of Highlanders bound for Topo in Columbia. Scottish immigrants could be found throughout Latin America from Chile north to Mexico during the nineteenth century.

**Publications.** *Scots in Latin America* (David Dobson, Baltimore, 2003); *Scots on the River Plate, and Their Churches* (J. Dodds, Buenos Ayres, 1897).

## SCOTS IN AFRICA

Africa attracted relatively few Scots settlers, apart from explorers, missionaries, and merchants. The main area of Scottish settlement was in what became South Africa. In 1815, during the Napoleonic Wars, the Dutch colony at the Cape of Good Hope was absorbed into the British Empire, which opened it to Scottish immigrants. Cape Colony had originally been a Dutch settlement servicing Dutch ships bound for Asia. The first Scots there were probably soldiers and sailors, with civilian settlement starting in 1817.

Emigration from Scotland to southern Africa was small-scale until the introduction of assisted passages in the mid-nineteenth century—to illustrate this, in 1841 only 55 people arrived from the British Isles, but after the introduction of assisted passages the numbers soared, reaching 1,342 in 1849. Immigration from the UK to South Africa only became significant when gold was discovered in the Transvaal, and diamonds were discovered at Kimberley in the 1880s.

**Publications**. *Scots in South Africa, 1772-1914* (John McKenzie, Manchester, 2013).

# SCOTS IN ASIA

Scots could be found in Asia from the early seventeenth century onward as mariners, soldiers, merchants, and administrators, predominantly in the service of the English East India Company but also of the Dutch East India Company and those of Sweden and Denmark. The first Scot known to be in China was William Carmichael in Portuguese service in Macao around 1600, while Henry Schanks, a mariner and merchant from Leith, had settled in Batavia, Dutch East Indies, by 1625. The East India Company had a monopoly of trade with India, which ended in 1813, and from 1858 the Crown administered British India.

During the eighteenth and early nineteenth century, the East India Company employed a significant number of Scots as administrators, surgeons, and military officers. Scots planters and merchants were attracted in significant numbers to India during the Victorian period. Scottish companies were prominent in Asia during the nineteenth century, firms such as Jardine Matheson, which at one point controlled two-thirds of China's external trade. Another prominent Scottish firm was McKinnon, McKenzie, and Company, which was involved mainly in shipping. The HSBC was founded by Scots.

Japan was closed to foreign settlement until the mid-nineteenth century and only those from Scotland with special skills seem to have located there, men like Henry Brunton, who constructed lighthouses there between 1868 and 1876. Without doubt, the most influential Scot there was Thomas Blake Glover (1838-1911), who arrived in Nagasaki as an agent of Jardine Matheson and Company, tea merchants, in 1859. Two years later he established his own business there and was prominent in developing its shipbuilding and mining. Glover's shipbuilding enterprise eventually developed into the Mitsubishi Company of Japan.

**Publications.** *The Corn Chest for Scotland, the Scots in India* (A. M. Cain, Edinburgh, 1986); *The Scots and China, 1750-2000* (I. Wotherspoon, Charleston, 2013); *Directory of Scots in Asia, 1600-1900* (David Dobson, St. Andrews, 2008).

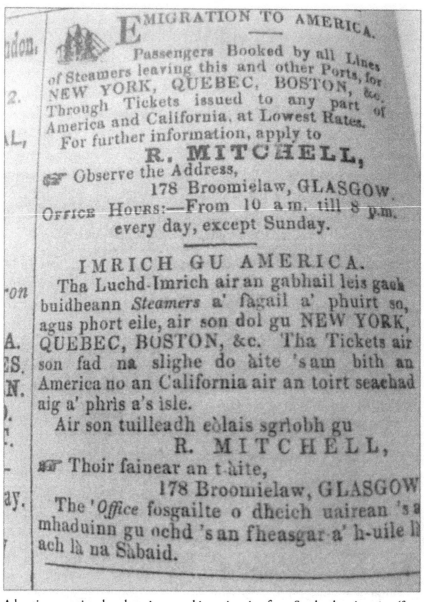

Advertisement aimed at those interested in emigrating from Scotland to America *(from The Gaelic Advertiser)*

# SCOTS IN NORTH AMERICA

Scottish immigration to North America was relatively limited in the seventeenth century. Attempts had been made to establish a colony in Nova Scotia in the 1620s but were unsuccessful, though settlements in South Carolina and East New Jersey, both within English jurisdiction, survived. Only a few thousand Scots settled within the Swedish, Dutch, and English colonies along the east coast of America, some of whom arrived in chains as prisoners banished to the American Plantations. These prisoners consisted of felons and prisoners of war captured by Oliver Cromwell or Covenanters who had resisted the religious policies of the Stuart kings. Religious persecution of the Quakers (Society of Friends) in Scotland persuaded most of them to move to East New Jersey in the 1680s.

The political union of Scotland and England in 1707 opened up the English colonies to Scottish merchants, shipping, and emigrants. The first sizable groups of Scots to go to the American colonies in the eighteenth century were Jacobite prisoners of war taken after the failure of the rebellion of 1715 and those after the failed rebellion in 1746. Commercial opportunity in the tobacco trade resulted in Glasgow merchants and their servants settling around the Chesapeake Bay. Due to the Navigation Acts and geographical reasons, Glasgow became the most important port in the British Isles engaged in the tobacco trade. Most of the tobacco was exported to markets in western Europe, while local industry was developed to produce goods for the American market.

The Seven Years War, 1756 to 1763, known in America as the French and Indian War, was the cause of substantial settlement of Scottish soldiers in colonial America. The British Government was keen to settle territories captured from the French in Canada and offered land grants to encourage settlement there and in other areas, such as the Mohawk Valley of upper New York. In the 1760s and early 1770s, there was substantial emigration from Scotland, particularly from the Highlands; for example, over four hundred MacDonell clansmen sailed from Fort William bound for New York in 1773. Lowland emigrants were heading for ports from Savannah north to New England, generally as individuals or small family groups. Notable exceptions were the Scots-America Company of Farmers and the United Company of Farmers for the Shires of Perth and Stirling, which organized the shipment and settlement of large numbers of their members in what is now Vermont, on the eve of the American Revolution. The American Revolution had a major impact on the Scots colonists in America. Most were Loyalists, and many of them found it advisable to move elsewhere. The majority of Scottish Loyalists and soldiers were granted land in Canada after 1783. Some moved to the British West Indies and others returned home. However, a number chose to live in the United States. In the aftermath of the American Revolution, the British Government discouraged immigration to the U.S. in favor of settlement in Canada.

Scottish settlement in Canada, despite the attempts of the 1620s, really began after 1763, when the French possessions of Acadia and Quebec were ceded to the British Crown. The French colonies were renamed Nova Scotia, New Brunswick, and Prince Edward Island, with Quebec becoming Upper and Lower Canada. These territories had to be settled quickly, so the British Government granted land to former soldiers and American Loyalists there. Among the army units concerned were the 77th (Montgomery's Highlanders) Regiment, the 78th (Fraser's Highlanders) Regiment, the 42nd (Black Watch) Regiment, and the King's Royal Regiment of New York. This generated further emigration from Scotland, as their families, friends, and neighbors left to settle in Canada too. A few former soldiers became fur traders, often based in Montreal. The fact that Catholics had a greater security in Canada under the Act of 1774 seems to have encouraged Catholic Highlanders to choose Canada as a destination; for example, in 1785 Father Alexander McDonnel brought over five hundred of his parishioners. From the late seventeenth century onward, the Hudson Bay Company, though based in London, increasingly depended on Scots, especially Orcadians, to man their stores.

**Publications.** "Seventeenth-Century Scottish Communities in the Americas" (David Dobson, in *Scottish Communities Abroad in the Early Modern Period*, A. Grosjean and Steve Murdoch, Leiden, 2005); *Scotland's Empire, 1600-1815* (T. M. Devine, London, 2003); *Scotland and America, 1600-1800* (Alexander Murdoch, London, 2010); *Scottish Emigration to Colonial America, 1607-1785* (David Dobson, Athens, Ga.,

2004); *Voyagers to the West, a Passage in the Peopling of America on the Eve of the Revolution* (Bernard Bailyn, New York, 1986); *Cargoes of Despair and Hope* (I. Adams and M. Somerville, Edinburgh, 1993); *The People's Clearance, 1770-1815* (J. M. Bumstead, Edinburgh, 1982); *Scotus Americanus* (W. R. Brock, Edinburgh, 1982); *The Scottish Tradition in Canada* (W. Stanford Reid, Toronto, 1977); *Tam Blake & Co., the Story of the Scots in America* (Jim Hewitson, Edinburgh, 1993).

## SCOTS IN THE WEST INDIES

Scotland has had direct social and economic links with the West Indies for around four hundred years, from the time when Spanish power there began to wane. The first vessel known to have sailed from Scotland to the Caribbean was the *Janet of Leith,* which left in 1611. Settlement by Scots began when Scot James Kay, Earl of Carlisle, was appointed Proprietor of Barbados in 1626, which led to a handful of Scots settling there. The English spread from Barbados along the chain of islands known as the Leewards and the Windwards, and in 1655 they took Jamaica from Spanish control. Settlers and servants were in great demand, which was partly met by indentured servants, including some Scots, being shipped to the colonies in the West Indies. However, the majority of Scots in the Caribbean at that time were transportees banished there. These included prisoners of war sent by Oliver Cromwell, Covenanters considered as rebels, and criminals taken from the jails of Edinburgh. There were also some of the survivors of the disastrous Darien Scheme and a small number of migrants from Edinburgh and Glasgow. Therefore, during the seventeenth century small numbers of Scots could be found in the English and Dutch colonies in the Caribbean. Those in the Dutch islands were probably two-stage migrants, who had initially settled in the Netherlands.

After the union of Scotland and England in 1707, all restrictions on trade between Scotland and the English colonies were lifted. This led to a significant expansion of Scottish trade in the West Indies, and settlement there by Scots increased. In 1763 the French ceded many of their Caribbean islands to Great Britain, including Dominica, Grenada, Tobago, and St. Vincent. Soon families in Scotland and elsewhere in the British Isles were investing in plantations in these islands, bringing in skilled agricultural overseers, millwrights, and surgeons. The planters grew sugar cane, cotton, and tobacco; they also produced rum, which was shipped to Britain for processing and then sold in European markets. Trading links were also established with American ports, which in turn led to families migrating between the mainland and the islands. The main Scottish burgh to benefit from these economic links was Glasgow, though others participated. The actual number of Scots who moved to the Caribbean is difficult to assess. Some were transients, only there temporarily, who after making their fortunes returned to Scotland. Some died prematurely due to disease and the climate, others settled there permanently.

**Publications**. *Soujourners in the Sun: Scottish Migrants in Jamaica and the Chesapeake, 1740-1800* (A. L. Karras, Ithaca, 1992); *Scotland's Empire, 1600-1815* (T. M. Devine, London, 2003); *Scotland, the Caribbean and the Atlantic World, 1750-1820* (D. J. Hamilton, Manchester, 2005); *Scotland, Darien and the Atlantic World, 1698-1700* (J. Orr, Edinburgh, 2018); *Barbados and Scotland, Links 1627-1877* (David Dobson, Baltimore, 2005); *Scots in Jamaica, 1655-1855* (David Dobson, Baltimore, 2011); *Scots in the West Indies, 1707-1857*, two volumes (David Dobson, Baltimore, 1998, 2006); *The Original Scots Colonists of Early America: Caribbean Supplement, 1611-1707* (David Dobson, Baltimore, 1999).

## VICTORIAN ERA EMIGRATION

The expansion of the British Empire during the nineteenth century opened up a wide range of destinations for emigrants from Scotland. While most Scottish emigration was in territories under British rule, Scots could be found in virtually every corner of the world, from Argentina to Hawaii. The reasons for such emigration were complex but included religious and political persecution, economic and social opportunities, and military service abroad. Immigration, both transatlantic and to the Antipodes, had one general common feature—movement from the Highlands tended to be in *family* groups whereas that from the Lowlands was usually by *individuals*. An unusual feature of Scottish emigration in the nineteenth century was that the average emigrant was no longer a common laborer but was more likely to be a skilled or semi-skilled artisan from either an urban or rural background. Also, as the century progressed, certainly after 1860, more emigrants came from the Lowlands than from the Highlands.

What made Scottish emigrants different from most European emigrants of the Victorian period was that they generally had industrial and commercial skills that were in demand at home and were not rural workers who were surplus to the need of an agrarian society. There were notable exceptions to this generalization, particularly those who emigrated as a result of the Highland Clearances. Most Scottish emigrants of the period were skilled, educated workers from urban backgrounds whose expertise was in great demand in the rapidly industrializing cities of North America. The level of annual emigration reflected the fluctuations of the trade cycle during the century. Immigrants to the United States have been relatively well recorded, with records dating from around 1820, most of which are accessible online. The equivalent records for Canada date from nearly a generation later.

***Publications****. To the Ends of the Earth: Scotland's Global Diaspora, 1750-2010* (T. M. Devine, London, 2011); *The Scottish Diaspora* (T. Bueltmann, A. Hinson, and G. Morton, Edinburgh, 2013); *The Modern Scottish Diaspora* (M. S. Leith and D. Sim, Edinburgh, 2014).

# Appendix

## FAMILY HISTORY SOCIETIES IN SCOTLAND

Aberdeen and North East Scotland FHS, 158-164 King Street, Aberdeen, AB24 5BD **(https://anesfhs.org.uk/)**

Borders FHS, 52 Overhaugh Road, Galashiels, TD1 1DP **(http://bordersfhs.org.uk)**

FHS of Buchan, 77 Broad Street, Peterhead, AB42 1JL **(https://www.buchanroots.scot/)**

Caithness FHS, 6 Clayock, Halkirk, KW12 6UZ **(http://caithnessfhs.org.uk/)**

Central Scotland FHS, 4 Fir Lane, Larbert, FK5 3LW **(https://csfhs.org.uk/)**

Dumfries and Galloway FHS, 9 Glasgow Street, DG29AF **(https://dgfhs.org.uk)**

East Ayrshire FHS, The Dick Institute, Kilmarnock, KA1 3BU **(http://www.eastayrshirefhs.co.uk/)**

Fife FHS, 33 Crossgate, Cupar, KY15 5AS **(https://fifefhs.org/)**

Glasgow and West of Scotland FHS, Unit 13, 32 Mansfield Street, Glasgow, G1 5QP (http://gwsfhs.org.uk)

Highland FHS, c/o Highland Archive and Registration Centre, Inverness, IV3 5SS (http://highlandfamilyhistorysociety.org)

Lanarkshire FHS, North Lanarkshire Heritage Centre, High Road, Motherwell, ML1 3HU (http://lanarkshirefhs.org)

Lothians FHS, c/o Lasswade Centre Library, Eskdale Drive, Bonnyrigg, EH19 2LA (http://www.lothiansfamilyhistorysociety.co.uk/)

North Ayrshire FHS, Largs Library, 26 Allanpark Street, Largs, KA30 9AG (http://northayrshirefhs.org.uk)

Orkney FHS, Orkney Library & Archives, 44 Junction Road, Kirkwall, KW15 1AG (https://orkneyfhs.co.uk)

Renfrewshire FHS, 51 Mathie Crescent, Gourock, PA19 1YU (http://renfrewshirefhs.co.uk)

Scottish Genealogy Society, 15 Victoria Terrace, Edinburgh, EH1 2JL (https://www.scotsgenealogy.com)

Shetland FHS, 6 Hillhead, Lerwick, ZE1 OEJ (https://shetland-fhs.org.uk)

Tay Valley FHS, 178-181 Princes Street, Dundee, DD4 6DQ (https://www.tayvalleyfhs.org.uk)

Troon, Ayrshire FHS, Troon Library, Troon, KA10 6EF (https://www.troonayrshirefhs.org.uk)

West Lothian FHS, 21 Willow Park, Fauldhouse, Bathgate, EH47 9HN (https://wlfhs.org.uk)

# Index

# Surname Index

## LIST OF SURNAMES MENTIONED IN THE TEXT

9 780806 321134